Searching for Guan Yin

SEARCHING FOR GUAN YIN

SARAH E. TRUMAN

WHITE PINE PRESS / BUFFALO, NEW YORK

White Pine Press
P.O. Box 236
Buffalo, New York 14201
www.whitepine.org

Publication of this book was made possible by support
with public funds from the New York State Council
on the Arts, a State Agency.

Acknowledgements: Thank you Dennis Maloney for inspiring me to
compile my Chinese experiences into a book; and to Clea McDougall,
without whose help I would never have organized my thoughts and written
it. Thank you Eliza Marciniak and Michael Tetreau for copyediting and
for the Real Ale in London. Many thanks to all of my wise friends in
China and beyond for supporting me on this journey!

I acknowledge with gratitude the Ontario
Arts Council Writers' Works in Progress
Grant.

Author's Note: The events and the people described in this book are
real. Some names and circumstances have been modified to protect the
identity of certain individuals or aid the storyline.

First Edition
ISBN: 978-1-935210-28-3
Library of Congress Control Number: 2011931991
Printed and bound in the United States of America.

Contents

To Sri, my best teacher and friend.

Chapter 1

The Antique Market (Nanjing)

*Introducing Guan Yin Pusa, China, some grave robbers
and Chinese drinking games*

It is the season of falling leaves. An autumn sun hangs in the sky and the crisp air has driven away Nanjing's usual scent. I walk down a narrow lane toward the center of the city, hemmed in between tanned walls and black-shingled roofs. The lane is too narrow for much motorized traffic and is quiet except for the squeaking of bikes and giggles of a couple of older women playing a cramped game of badminton.

Up ahead, a man pushing a bike piled high with a heavy load lurches forward. Something about the way he moves makes me pause, then move aside so as not to get in his way. He sweats under the weight and stares straight ahead as he approaches.

I'm used to seeing people pushing and pulling peculiar loads through the narrow lanes—sludge from restaurants, bricks, fowl, recycling, you name it. But this is the first time I've seen someone transporting fish tanks. The man's bike is stacked high—twelve fish tanks, on tiered platforms on either side of the back wheel, filled to the brim with water and colorful fishes swaying with each step. It's remarkable that the whole thing hasn't capsized onto the dusty pavement. Sunlight streams through the tanks, casting tiny fish shadows and translucent ripples onto the ground. The fish swim back and forth in rainbow colors and fluorescent stripes, unaware their watery world teeters on the back of a rickety bicycle.

The fish tanks disappear around the bend and I continue down the lane until it meets a larger street, broad, lined with shops—bike shops with shiny new bikes in bright colors; a TV shop, stacked full of crazy old TVs; a meat shop specializing in fried pig skins, which make me gag; a metal parts shops with pipes for plumbing and rebar protruding into the street next to a store selling bulk grains, beans and nuts. This street is much louder and busier than the little lane—like I advanced thirty years by turning a corner. Bikes, rickshaws, auto rickshaws, cars and trucks honk their way down the road beneath a rainbow of flags announcing an upcoming festival. There's never any room to walk on the sidewalks on these kinds of streets because of the stuff piled everywhere, so I negotiate the traffic and other pedestrians, all of whom sound like they're screaming as they converse with each other. A man dressed in the fancy leather dress shoes that everyone in China wears (construction workers included) plucks a duck outside of one tiny restaurant. In front of the next, a woman in a bright red jacket with lime green arm protectors throws a live fish onto the cement, seemingly to paralyze it before chopping off its head and scaling it on the asphalt.

At the intersection, the street connects with a wide boulevard lined with trees and transitions into another China—the China of the Sheraton hotels and Western restaurants. There are a growing number of such streets in the city—the rate of construction is staggering, with workers imported from the countryside who work around the clock on high-rises and sleep in tenements beside the canal. But the reality of China as a third-world nation still lurks around the edges of these flashy new buildings and oozes in through the feeder streets.

Waiting for the lights to change, a chubby man in a business suit stands beside me. He clears his throat several times before expectorating a large gob onto the pavement. His spit lies between us in a phlegmy blob, reminiscent of a broken egg with different colors and textures. Examining it for a moment I realize that after two months in the People's Republic of China I may have finally arrived.

❧

I've always had a strong connection to China—ever since I was a child. Driving through Toronto's Chinatown I would get dizzy from the sights, the sounds and the language written above the bright shops. Sometimes it would be too much and I'd duck down below the window level of the car, cover my eyes and hold my breath so as not to take it in. When I went to the University of Toronto I often walked through Chinatown and paused at windows, overwhelmed by the amount of manufactured knickknacks for sale. I swooned twice in Chinatown and had to be carted to a nearby park to convalesce.

Although I had a strong reaction to the sights and sounds of Chinatown, I always went back because of my affinity to Guan Yin: Chinatown was chock-full of Guan Yin statues.

Guan Yin, Quan Yin, or Kuan Yin is the Chinese name for *Avalokiśvara*, the Indian bodhisattva who perceives sounds and beholds the world with ease. He is classically affiliated with light imagery and unbounded compassion. Some scholars date his origin back to early Shivaite lineage (the tradition of the Hindu god Shiva). But he is mainly affiliated with Buddhist scriptures of the Mahayana tradition that regard him as a manifestation of compassion. A bodhisattva is a "realized being" or "energy" that forgoes nirvana or final liberation in order to help others. *Avalokiśvara* is particularly renowned for his compassionate vow to return to the world until every living being has achieved realization.

When Buddhism arrived in China, *Avalokiśvara*'s compassionate nature resonated with the Chinese psyche. His popularity flourished and in time he was worshiped in every level of society from the Emperor's Palace to muddy grottos of fishing villages.

He even managed to switch genders somewhere along the way, and Guan Yin is now usually thought of as a she in China. Some people believe that the popularity of a Daoist deity—the Queen of Heaven—may have persuaded the Buddhists to come up with a female deity. Others say that Christian images of the Virgin Mary that entered China in the seventh century may have influenced the Buddhist iconography. Others say that the Tibetan goddess of compassion, Tara, may be the cause of the gender switch. I'm more inclined to believe that the human mind, when thinking of compassion, naturally thinks of something feminine, and Guan Yin is a manifestation of compassion, so it makes sense that she's feminine.

She is known for her ability to use "skillful means"—whatever expediency suggests—to liberate those who call on her for help. In the *Lotus Sutra*, the Buddha promises that even calling Guan Yin's name wholeheartedly is enough to be relieved of suffering. So devotees regularly chant Guan Yin's name and visualize and meditate on her form.

And her skillful means also enable Guan Yin to manifest herself in a variety of forms to help devotees. There are scriptures from India and China and hundreds of personal accounts of her manifesting as everything from a horse to an old man to a multiheaded being with a thousand arms and eyes to the more popular image of a beautiful woman in flowing white gowns.

You could say that there are as many descriptions of Guan Yin as there are minds to conceive her. And on that note, I have a very specific form in mind when I think of Guan Yin. For years, I've dreamed and had visualizations of her as a tall white figure—at least ten feet tall—with flowing gowns, large eyes and hands. In dreams and visualizations I've encountered her in a variety of locations, from nebulous sparkling space to fiery planes to laser-like grids. But more often, I see her on a cliff, by a large body of water, next to a Chinese-style house.

In some myths, Guan Yin is said to live in the East Sea on an island near a purple bamboo grove and a cave of tidal sound. It is on the tenuous belief in such a place that I've come to China searching for Guan Yin. The idea has been percolating for a few years, and several people warned me that China is an unforgiving country to visit, and that Guan Yin isn't an actual being. But that didn't deter me. I decided that I had to come here and see for myself what Guan Yin is and is not and what China is and is not.

Getting up the nerve to leave my life in Canada and come to China was a slow process—like the gradual heating of water that suddenly boils, turns to vapor. I had spent three years living at a yoga retreat center and was planning to stay on for another year when I was sitting in meditation one night and heard a loud voice say "GO!" I had the image of myself in Montreal and then China.

So I did move to Montreal and worked as an editor. At night I did the regular city things of someone in her twenties—played music, practiced tai chi and drank at the local pubs. I was slowly lulled into the complacency that many of us develop when working in a city. But at the same time I was rallying against it: I refused to buy a bed and slept on the floor—I knew that sooner or later I would be leaving. I was just waiting for a sign. It didn't dawn on me until one winter's night when my co-workers were heading to the pub that I'd already had a "sign." It was up to me to decide to go to China and to make it happen. So that night, instead of going out to the pub, I went online and found a job as an editor and teacher in Nanjing.

I'm in charge of editing the "Chinglish" versions of texts for the university. "Chinglish" is the slang name given to translations of Chinese into English. I take the Ching-lish version and re-write it in English. I'm also in charge of teaching "Oral English" to two hundred students and "Western Culture" to fifty students. The Western Culture class is based around a book that makes sweeping statements such as "Thirty percent of the West is on drugs" and "It is unsafe to walk on the streets in America because you will get shot," statements that may or may not be true, but it's not my job to argue with the text. I'm to teach from the book and only periodically fill in my perspective for "color."

I live in a gray cement six-story building like many of the residential blocks here in Nanjing. My apartment is number 411. This seemed fine to me until I learned that number 4 in Chinese has the same pronuncia-tion as the word "death." And the number 1, when said aloud is pronounced "yao," which sounds the same as "to want." So my apartment is "death want want." My first day here when I woke up I was so excited to be in China that I opened my blinds and window and stuck my head out to wave at a woman in the next apartment block. She promptly closed her window then drew the blinds and didn't wave back. She wasn't as excited as I was to be in China.

But I like my life here. I get up in the morning and pedal my squeaky bike down dusty lanes. I watch the streets come alive in the pale pink sunlight and marvel at how many people are already up and functional at six a.m. My tai chi class meets in Mochu Park, in an open area between gingko trees and swaying willows. There are several hundred other people practicing with various teachers each morning—all in swaying tai chi clothes of white, red, pink, and blue and in black slippers or bright white sneakers. Some practice with fans, others with swords or canes. Old men and women walk their birds to the park in small bamboo cages and hang them in the trees. The multicolored birds sing pretty songs and serenade our practice.

On the way home each morning I stop for breakfast on the street. Breakfast is my favorite meal in China. By 7:30 the laneways outside of the university's gates are filled with vendors cooking over charcoal piles. Some stack towers of bamboo steamers full of steamed buns, others stir pots of warm soy milk, but my favorite are the *youtiao* makers. *Youtiao* is a long greasy fried bread stick, kind of like a donut without the sugar. What the vendors do is take some batter, cook it into a thin crepe, then fill it with steamed vegetables, spicy sauce and roll a *youtiao* inside. The result is a crispy, savory, deliciously greasy treat that I munch while watching the morning exercises at the university. At 7:45 every morning, the undergraduates line up on the rubber football field dressed in matching school tracksuits. The teachers stand in front and go through an exercise routine to a national sports theme song.

A voice comes over the top and calls out directions: "Arms out, arms up, stretch left, stretch right!" and several hundred students in frighteningly straight rows follow along.

Needless to say, I haven't run into Guan Yin or her house here in this context. And I can't very well tell people that I'm in China looking for a bodhisattva. So I keep it to myself for the most part. Mine's a solo journey, except for my sandalwood pocket Guan Yin who comes everywhere with me. I had a great fear that she would be discovered at the airport and confiscated on my entry into China. I actually considered swallowing her to smuggle her in. That wasn't necessary. Pocket Guan Yin is smooth, smells good, and has a little rough spot where her hand broke off and was glued on three separate times in Canada until I finally lost it for good. I know it's strange and is probably considered sacrilege by some—keeping bodhisattvas in pockets, breaking their arms off, treating them as "dolls," as I've been accused of doing—but I've been happy to find that here in China many people carry jade talismans for protection, around their necks, in their pockets, on their belts. Maybe Pocket Guan Yin and I have finally found our place.

❧

The antique market lies across the busy street on the grounds of an old temple—its high terra-cotta walls and teeming square warm in the sunlight.

This isn't my first time at the market. I come most Sundays since I discovered it. There are about fifty vendors in the main square of the temple and about twenty more permanent store-like stalls. Sometimes another fifty vendors set up on blankets outside the gate displaying jade, coins, pornographic carvings on ivory slats, vases, leathers and in some cases pieces of rare animals such as tiger and bear paws for outlawed traditional Chinese medical practices.

I stop at a stall stacked high with intricate wood carvings that look like they've been salvaged from torn-down temples or old homes.

"Mai bu mai?" the vendor asks.

"Bu mai," I respond, he frowns and I continue, stopping at several booths but not stopping long enough to engage with the vendors. I'm looking for something specific today. A statue of Guan Yin for my altar, something special—antique.

Since arriving here in China, I've encountered myriad Guan Yin paraphernalia: Guan Yin flashing red light dangly things hanging from the rearview mirror in taxis, Guan Yins in water that if you shake them upside down will be showered in little plastic coins symbolizing wealth, Guan Yin stickers in gum machines. At first I thought that kitsch and rebuilt statues were what Guan Yin has been reduced to here in modern China. But Guan Yin will manifest in any form to help devotees, so maybe the modern mind likes trinkets. Or maybe all I see is trinkets, and I'm missing the point. It's difficult to be objective about something as personal as my relationship with Guan Yin.

Although this is an "antique" market, there's a lot of modern junk posing as antiques to sift through, particularly when it comes to statues. Many antiques were destroyed during the Cultural Revolution when anything representative of the old culture or religion was outlawed. I can never quite find what I'm looking for. Plus, I'm a terrible shopper.

I stop to admire a jade carving of Guan Yin, feel its cool weight in my hands and begin to get dizzy. The vendor yelling "Mai bu mai?" heightens the dizziness. I put the jade carving down and move away from the stall. A tiny older woman in a blue Chairman Mao suit jabs me in the back so she can get through the tangle of people—the characteristic shove that many older Chinese people give when trying to pass through a small area. It's not aggressive, just cold and pointed, usually in the kidneys. I have the urge to return the favor but I know it wasn't personal.

I've come to see that the statues were what was making me dizzy in Chinatown—something happens to my mind when I'm in the presence of certain images of Guan Yin.

I get this high-pitched buzzing in my ears and feel like I'm going to fall into the statue. My friend warned me before I came to China that I would probably faint when I saw all the Guan Yins here. I haven't fainted yet, but I sometimes come close. I reach into my pocket for my Pocket Guan Yin instead—she doesn't make me dizzy. I clutch her tiny form and walk through the gates into the main temple grounds where I'm supposed to meet my friend, Jimmy.

It is quieter and cool in the shade inside the temple walls. There's a sea of things to buy but I see only statues.

This is how they always appear, lined up like an army watching me watching them: the more I look, the more I see—Guan Yins everywhere, some with vases in hand representing her compassionate nectar, others with lotuses or infants. They're mostly modern ones though, not what I'm looking for today.

"Hey, over here," Jimmy calls from in front of a booth. He sticks out in a crowd because he's tall for a Chinese man and always wears an undone plaid button-up shirt with a concert T-shirt underneath like he's from the Seattle grunge scene. But he's not. He's from Gansu province and "Jimmy" is the English name he gave himself after none other than Jimi Hendrix. Jimmy plays guitar and has a wild streak, hates communism and Chairman Mao, and is trying to get out of the mandatory communist weekend classes that he's been forced to take since arriving here in Nanjing as a new teacher.

And he knows about Guan Yin and I. In fact, he's one of the only people I've told about my reasons for coming to China. After he told me how much he loves rock and roll, I felt like I could confide in him. Although he doesn't believe in Guan Yin and can't understand why I came to China looking for her, he continues to support my search and often accompanies me on my trips to temples and antique markets.

We move toward the side stalls where old scrolls and calligraphy dangle from hand-carved screens and jade and bronze statues peek from dusty shelves. A couple of the vendors sit in front of their shops smoking. I recognize them and they recognize me. One man begins talking to me in unintelligible Chinese vowels and roller-coaster tones as we approach. Jimmy seems to find it funny and laughs with the vendor man.

"What's he saying?" I ask.

"He's calling you the girl who always looks but never buys," laughs Jimmy. "What about this one?" he holds a porcelain Guan Yin statue with a bad paint job.

"That's not an antique. It was probably made in some factory in Guangdong last month," I say.

"I don't understand why it has to be an antique—why not have something clean and new?" Jimmy asks.

"Because," I say. "The longer I'm in China, the

more I realize that I'm just another one of those for-eigners who has come here looking for a China that is lost—the China of romantic temples, great sages, statues and philosophy, the China of my imagination—a China that probably never existed in the first place." And the irony of my being unable to accept a "modern" Guan Yin statue is not lost on me.

"Ni zhao jiu de Guan Yin?" says a voice over my shoulder.

"Dui," I respond, assuming the small man with several teeth missing is another vendor.

"Wo you. Lai lai," he says.

Jimmy and I follow him, knowing that he probably doesn't have anything we're interested in. When he leads us clear out of the temple complex onto the main street Jimmy says, "I don't know if we should keep following him. He might be a robber."

"He doesn't look like a robber," I say.

"How do you know what a robber looks like?"

We wait at the intersection and the man lights a cigarette. He offers me one and I decline. I put my hand into my jeans to feel Pocket Guan Yin, making sure she hasn't fallen out somewhere along the way. Jimmy accepts a cigarette and seems resigned to follow the man.

I don't know this section of the city. We leave the larger streets and begin weaving down the narrow lanes. I try to keep my sense of direction as we hurry past people sitting on stoops preparing supper and chatting. The narrower the lanes, the darker they become. I size statue man up: he is rather small with his little beige jacket and black dress pants and patent leather shoes. I'm at least a head taller than he, and Jimmy and I surely could take him in a fight if need be.

"But what if he's with a gang?"

I slow down and he grabs my sleeve, beckoning me forward saying, "Guan Yin, Guan Yin lai lai." His eyes are shifty but not cruel. Jimmy shrugs and we continue to follow the man down another laneway.

The lane, with its miniature houses, is marked for progress—the writing literally on the wall. The character "chui" is spray-painted in blue on every building. I've seen it happening all over the city. It goes like this: "chui" is painted on a building and a week afterward the entire block is leveled in the name of a beautification campaign. What unnerves me the most about the construction is the displacement inherent in it. Many of these side streets are marked for demolition because they're in prime development areas—close to downtown. Sadly, many of the older buildings are houses, and I often see families living amid the rubble—they string tarps, pile bricks, cook meals and wash their hair where their houses used to stand. Apparently, they are offered relocation to apartment housing elsewhere in the city, but they don't want to leave their homes.

We stop in front of a rooming house. The door off the lane is like a prison door with bars. There's also a prison window with no glass, just bars. The doorway opens into a long concrete rectangle with a hole in the roof creating a dingy courtyard. On one side of the courtyard is the bathroom—I can smell it from here. On the other side are about ten doors, likely to individual rooms. Although it hasn't rained for days, the half-covered courtyard is moist, the way most places in Nanjing are moist—oozing. Even indoors in the smaller restaurants, the floor is always slightly damp, just damp enough that you don't want to lift your feet too high whilst walking for fear of slipping, so everyone slides along on the tiles.

The place seems sketchy but there are quite a few people around. There are always a few people around in China—it doesn't really matter where you go, there's always someone watching. Jimmy shrugs again and we enter the courtyard, sliding our feet along the tiles toward the man's room. He lives in room number six, directly across the courtyard from the bathroom. He opens the door, shuffles us inside and closes the door behind us. The room is about ten by twelve feet and ridiculously full of boxes—from floor to ceiling, on the bed, covering the window.

"What the hell?" I say. He smiles his toothless smile.

He opens one of the larger boxes and lifts out a seated Guan Yin in the Royal Ease pose. She has an elaborate headdress with the Buddha nestled in her hair. She's made of fine metalwork and has delicate hands in *mudra*—a symbolic hand gesture. She looks old.

He continues, opening box after box of antique Guan Yins and Buddhas, all of them unique, all of them refined—some standing but most of them sitting. That far-away music begins to fill my head; I lean against the wall to keep upright.

This is more Guan Yins than I've ever seen in one spot. Part of me wants to collect them all, rent a truck and drive them to safety somewhere. But another part of me knows that they are merely statues and Guan Yin doesn't need to be saved.

"I told you he was a robber," smiles Jimmy.

"You thought he was going to rob us!"

"He's still a robber."

These statues are likely all stolen from god knows where. A temple. A grave? Maybe they were hidden during the Cultural Revolution to preserve them. Now they're piled in boxes in this dank room. I wonder where he plans to sell them; he clearly can't set up a stall in the market—maybe he is a supplier and sells to overseas dealers. It feels like a sleazy operation. I begin to have mixed feelings about accruing statues. How is it that objects of worship can turn into commodities? Does everything have a price?

There's a knock on the door and Statueman lets another small man in—he has the same shoes and dress pants as Statueman, but a blue jacket with the word "fission" written across the chest. I get the feeling that this is more than a one-man operation. They both light cigarettes. Fissionman offers Jimmy and I one. I decline and Jimmy accepts.

"Jimmy, tell Statueman that I'm looking for a 'standing Guan Yin.'"

Many Guan Yin statues depict her in seated positions, but I'm drawn to standing ones for some reason, maybe because when I've met her in dreams or visualizations she's usually standing.

He opens a few more boxes and finds a bronze standing Guan Yin, about a foot and a half high with an ornate gown and a large flaming halo. She stands on a lotus and looks almost Tibetan with those flames. She doesn't have the Buddha in her headdress as many statues usually do. Rather she has an image of her vase—her compassionate vase—in her headdress. She has compassion on her mind.

"Xi huan?" asks Fissionman, standing close enough that I can hear him breathing. Cigarette smoke swirls around the dangling lightbulb in the center of the room, making the scene more sinister. I'm beginning to feel a little cramped in here. I don't know how comfortable I am buying statues from these two. I don't know where they got them. All this effort to find old statues, and when I'm presented with them, I realize that old things have histories.

I decide to do an experiment: I have only 300 yuan in my pocket (about $45). If Statueman will sell her for 300, then I'm supposed to have her. Otherwise, I'll walk away.

"Wo gei ni 300 kuai qian," I say, not actually believing that Statueman will sell anything this rare and fine for that price.

Fissionman laughs and retorts, "1800."

I shrug and say goodbye to Statueman, Fissionman and take one last look at the Guan Yin statue—the thought of leaving her here tears my heart a little.

"Let's get out of here, Jimmy," I say and try to open the door. Fissionman holds it shut. I can feel adrenaline starting to flow through me. I don't like where this is going.

Statueman pulls out a Buddha statue, similar to Guan Yin with the same halo. He starts speaking quickly, trying to convince me to buy both statues because Guan Yin is a girl and the Buddha is a boy and I need both. He says he will give them to me for 1800 yuan.

Jimmy speaks some aggressive Chinese, pushes Fissionman aside, and we walk into the slippery courtyard, past the stinky bathroom and into the street.

"That was crazy," says Jimmy.

We're both breathing heavily and I have the urge to run. I can smell cigarette smoke on my clothes and my mind reels from the scene we just escaped. We walk quickly, but before we make it to the corner, I hear Statueman running after us. I almost break into a run, but Statueman starts yelling, "Guan Yin 300 kuai qian!"

He has Guan Yin in his hands and holds her out smiling. I take my three crisp red hundred-yuan bills and trade them for her.

"Man zou"—go slowly—Statueman says. Guan Yin is warm in my arms as we begin the walk home.

By the time we reach the main street the streetlights have come on. The amber light shines through the tree branches and makes sharp leafless shadows on the sidewalk.

Hanxi restaurant is a favorite haunt of mine. It is nuzzled among many other restaurants on an old small street near the university and has nothing notable about it, except that the owners know that I'm a vegetarian so they don't try to smuggle duck blood or giblets into my tofu. The restaurant is packed with students and other diners. Jimmy and I take the last empty table, beside the gray-white wall directly below the rattling fan. The waitress fills our cups with steaming jasmine tea and we wait for

Heathcliff—one of the university's administrators that Jimmy has cajoled me into dining with.

"So does this mean you can leave China, now that you have found Guan Yin?" asks Jimmy.

"I haven't exactly found her," I admit. "This is just a symbolic representation of her—of her compassion."

"So that isn't Guan Yin?"

"It is. But she's not just this form—she can take any form. This is just one of her countless forms."

"Then why couldn't you buy one of the other statues?"

"I'm not sure—mental block I guess." For someone who claims to understand Guan Yin's myriad manifestations, I sure am fixated on specific forms. I realize that this is a working area—I don't want to be a Guan Yin fundamentalist. I remember hearing a story once about some bodhisattvas who dressed like peasants and set up tea stalls on the side of a mountain path. When the pilgrims came by they were rude to the bodhisattvas because they thought they were peasants. I tell Jimmy. He looks confused.

"So Guan Yin could be a peasant instead of a statue?" he asks.

"Precisely. And I could even take this musing further and know that regardless of whether something is Guan Yin or not, in the end there's no difference anyway, because we all belong to non-being!"

"Then why look for Guan Yin at all?" Jimmy asks.

"Good question." I could ask myself: if Guan Yin can manifest in any form, why come all the way to China to look for her? And if we're all non-being anyway, why bother at all? I could come up with a logical explanation that I didn't need to come here; I could have found Guan Yin at home or not found her at home. But this isn't a logical equation—this is my life.

"What is that on the table?" Heathcliff asks before he sits down.

"Guan Yin," I say, wishing I'd dropped her off at home before coming to the restaurant. Heathcliff summons the waitress for a cup of tea and settles into his white plastic chair.

"You like Guan Yin. She's a famous Chinese goddess, you know." Heathcliff says. I want to correct him and say that she's actually a bodhisattva not a goddess but bite my tongue because who am I to get technical about what Guan Yin is or isn't.

Heathcliff was the first person I met in China. He picked me up at the airport in Shanghai and got lost while driving through the suburbs for about an hour before finding the highway to Nanjing. He is fluent in Latin and English, and his English is remarkable—considering he's never left China. He used to teach at the university but from the way he functions nowadays, I can see that he's on the rise to administrative power. He is a slender man with tidy hands and always dressed neatly in pleated dress pants and golf shirts (the non-uniform that most professional Chinese men have adopted). His English name came from the Heathcliff of *Wuthering Heights*.

"I think it is funny that you are Canadian and believe in Guan Yin. And now here in China people believe in Jesus. My mother is a Christian. She's very foolish," says Heathcliff. "We Chinese spent so many years furthering ourselves from superstitious religions, and now she has decided to follow one. And a foreign one at that."

Christianity has been trying in fits and starts for over a thousand years to enter China and it seems to be making slow progress. I have noticed several churches here in Nanjing, and there are supposedly more Christians than Buddhists in China, but the church doesn't share the historical weight or artistic presence of Buddhism. Although a foreign philosophy, Buddhism has a long history here and enjoyed the favors of emperors and imperial, philosophical and artistic influence for hundreds of years.

Several forms of Buddhism have developed in China during its two thousand years here. The most popular are Chan (known as Zen in Japan and the West) and the devotional Pure Land school. Guan Yin features big in Pure Land philosophy and is known as Amituo Fo's (Amitabha Buddha's) assistant. Both Guan Yin and Amituo Fo use their boundless merit to aid any devotee who calls on them. Some Purelanders in the past have chanted Guan Yin's or Amituo Fo's names for weeks on end, hoping to achieve merit through recitation. There are many stories of monks and nuns and lay people calling on Guan Yin or Amituo Fo and then being saved from perils or being on the verge of death and seeing visions of Pure Land. The idea of people from all classes and backgrounds being able to attain Pure Land has a large appeal in China.

I don't actually believe in Pure Land. It sounds too much like the Western idea of heaven to me. So in theory, I am partial to Chan or Zen. If only I weren't so hung up on Guan Yin's form.

Jimmy takes my Guan Yin statue and puts her at the end of the table against the wall so she now stands overlooking the meal.

"Namo Guan Yin!" Heathcliff jokes. I frown. Jimmy rolls his eyes at me and lights up a cigarette to hide behind.

"If you like Guan Yin, you should go to Putuo Shan," says Heathcliff, trying to be helpful. "You can visit there on your holidays, although it will be very busy on public holidays; you should go on a different day. It is Guan Yin's special island. I went once with my wife. We went swimming in the sea and saw the giant Guan Yin."

I've heard that Putuo Island, in the East China Sea, used to house over 200 monasteries but most of them were destroyed during the Cultural Revolution. Nowadays it's a military port and a tourist destination with karaoke bars, prostitution and trinkets. It is also still a pilgrimage site for thousands of Chinese Buddhists each year, but I'm afraid to visit for fear that my dream of finding Guan Yin and her house will be shattered for good.

"I plan to go, but not yet."

The food arrives: dishes of spicy tofu, fried lotus root and bitter melon for me and three meaty plates for Heathcliff and Jimmy. This is why there are sludge buckets out front of every restaurant. Chinese diners tend to order excessively because they want "variety of taste and color." We dig in, knowing we won't be able to eat everything.

"I think you would like some Jinling beer," says Heathcliff.

"No, I'm alright," I say.

"Just one bottle," he says and orders two. "You loved Chinese beer last time we went out." He smiles. Heathcliff has one of those voices that always sound mildly mocking or accusatory.

The waitress returns with three flimsy transparent plastic cups and two 750 ml bottles of Jinling beer—a light lager brewed in Nanjing.

"Gan bei," Heathcliff says in his particular tone.

"Gan bei," Jimmy and I chime. We all empty our glasses. "Gan bei" means "dry glass" and is a kind of toast that means you're supposed to drink the whole glass.

I went for supper with the university administrators to celebrate China's birthday on October 1st and was initiated into *gan bei*. Everything was red that night—red dragon cakes, red balloons, red banners, men and women in red suits. Slogans streaming from the ceiling. We had a private room with two private waitresses in red dresses serving us around a large white-clothed table covered in dishes, soups and nibbles. The restaurant was very classy, with stone floors and a river running through it with colorful fish and tiny bamboo bridges. In our private room, several of the administrators were challenging each other to *gan bei*, and I, being new to China followed suit, thinking it was proper etiquette. Consequently, I was part of the drinking contest that went on throughout supper. My saving grace was that Chinese beer is only 3.2 percent alcohol. I was used to Canadian beer and they couldn't keep up with me. I outdrank the university's president, the deputy director of foreign affairs, the head of the English department and several other administrators. This incident earned me a great deal of respect and a lot more trouble: I've been out several times since with various teachers and department heads and my reputation precedes me—as soon as we sit down, people start challenging me with *gan bei*. Sometimes here in China I feel like a monkey performing tricks.

Heathcliff refills our glasses and calls *gan bei* once more. Jimmy and I down our drinks, and I feel the warm rush of the alcohol through me.

"You are very strong," says Heathcliff proudly. I have the feeling this is going to be a long evening. Heathcliff refills our cups.

"Gan bei!"

I look at my Guan Yin statue for support and she seems to smile at me from across the table. Sometimes I think I'll never find her in this place we call China.

"Gan bei," I say and empty the glass.

Chapter 2

✧

The Despondency (Qi Xia Temple)
Nanjing and a visit to the 1000 Smashed Buddha Caves

The umbrella fixer always arrives about an hour before the rain comes. He unfurls his octagonal vinyl umbrella tops—bright colors against the pavement as the air moistens and the day darkens. I watch him from my window as people come by, invariably with a defective umbrella in their bags. They show him a bent corner or tear in the vinyl and leave their umbrella with him. He has a variety of metal supports, joints and patching techniques and can fix almost any umbrella.

I've never stopped to ask him how much he charges, but I can't imagine it's very much because a new umbrella only costs eight yuan. That said, a twenty-yuan umbrella would probably break after a couple of uses.

Maybe that's how the umbrella fixer stays in business—the built-in deficiency of mass production. He always disappears before the rain comes. He packed up this morning and sure enough, a few minutes later the mist descended.

Nanjing gives me the creeps when it rains. The city is hemmed in by a bend in the great Yangzi River, restricting its west and northern edges, and a large mountain in the east. These natural wonders do something to the wind and the *qi* of the city, creating a palpable stagnancy. The air, especially on a rainy day like today, feels thick and heavy—almost sinister.

Nanjing's history dates back more than 2500 years to the Yue City period. It has been the capital of "China" numerous times, from the third to the sixth century and in the early Ming Dynasty from 1368 to 1421. More recently Nanjing was the capital of the violent Christian Tai Ping movement (1853–64), during which it was renamed Tianjing—Heavenly Capital. The ruler of the "Heavenly Capital" was Hong Xiuquan, a peasant from the south who believed he was Jesus's younger brother. God had apparently told Hong that people were worshiping demons and it was his duty to scourge the place.

Hong had some egalitarian ideals, such as equal status for women, and believed in economic reforms, such as equal distribution of wealth, and managed to rally millions of supporters looking for a better way of life (many of them also had holy visions). But the heavenly kingdom unfurled, and Hong became more interested in harem life than in religion and politics and ultimately committed suicide.

Sun Yat Sen, the father of modern China and founder of the Republic of China, made Nanjing his capital from 1912 until his death in 1925, after which Cheng Kai Shek organized a coup in the south and took over the party. Cheng's Gumingdong then held Nanjing as capital until the Japanese, after occupying the north of China, sacked Nanjing in 1937. The city was reclaimed in 1946 by the Gumingdong but only held for three years before Chairman Mao and the People's Liberation Army (PLA) seized it and moved the capital to Beijing. The Gumingdong then fled to Taiwan and started a new country, leaving Nanjing as a place of the past.

History oozes through these streets. I met some people in Shanghai who told me that although it's only a four-hour train ride, they never visit Nanjing because it is haunted! The past presses in around the edges of my consciousness here. Sometimes when I'm riding my bike down a street, or even driving through town, I get the feeling that my existence is skating on the surface of a lake, unaware of the depths of the water underneath.

All of this came to a head yesterday at 11:00 a.m., the anniversary of the Japanese invasion of Nanjing: December 12, 1937. Every siren in the city screamed in a loud reminder. The sound made my flesh crawl, and the silence that followed the sirens was even more unsettling. Over 300,000 people were killed during the invasion. The city's gates were closed and the Chinese civilians were locked in with the Japanese soldiers, who raped, impaled and shot the women and men and then buried them in mass graves throughout the city. It was the Chinese government who locked the civilians inside, saying, "Better to die a broken piece of jade, than to live as a ceramic."

I was walking up the street yesterday when the sirens sounded. The dissonance they made sent an unsettled wave through my body. I live near one of the city's gates—its walls too tall to scale. I can't imagine what it must have felt like being locked *inside* the city with the opposing army.

There are no sirens today, just the light patter of rain as I sit beside a wall of steles—tall, granite, inscribed with poems overlooking a courtyard and one of the university's main doors. Students and teachers enter and exit the building with umbrellas. It's a war zone of umbrellas as the people leaving the building insist on opening their umbrellas before stepping through the double doorway into the courtyard. And those entering refuse to close their umbrellas until they're well inside the doors. As a result there's a tangle of colors, pushing and probing and poking, people slipping—and near gridlock. I'm surprised no one has been injured.

By the time Mrs. Du arrives, I've passed from being amused at the umbrella spectacle to being irritated at the bleak reality of group etiquette—and then to a settled indifference. I notice that my moods often swing in this way while watching Chinese culture at work. Within the span of a few minutes I can pass from elation into the depths of utter despondency and back again. Although I'm not able to control these mind swings, I do try to be conscious of their impermanent nature; otherwise I think China will drive me mad.

Mrs. Du wears a shiny red brocade jacket and carries a camera in her hand. "Good morning. Oh, you have no friends!" she says.

"I have friends, but the friend who's coming isn't here yet," I say. Mrs. Du has offered to escort my friend, Cristina, and me to visit Qi Xia monastery in the countryside for the afternoon. She sits beside me, swinging her legs as we wait for Cristina.

"Did you hear those sirens yesterday?" I ask.

"Of course. They ring them every year in reminder of the Japanese invasion. I hate the Japanese," she says decidedly.

She remains quiet for a minute and then continues. "The Japanese are cowards. When my cousin was a small boy in the countryside, a Japanese soldier who had been left behind when the army retreated came out of the bushes with his bayonet and asked my uncle to kill

41

him. He asked a young boy to kill him. Not because he was ashamed of what he did to our China, but because he was a coward and couldn't kill himself."

Her eyes are no longer kind and seem to burn. "Do you hate the Japanese?" she asks.

"No."

Before I came to China I knew vaguely about the war between China and Japan, but being here in present-day Nanjing I'm amazed to see how deep the hatred runs. The Japanese government still doesn't recognize the Nanjing massacre and the Chinese people are angry about it.

It's difficult to be a foreigner in a country with such a history and know my place, even in instances like this. Do I agree with Mrs. Du and decidedly dislike the Japanese for crimes committed in China before my time? Of course not. But it begs the question of preference: I have many convictions about cultural genocide in Tibet and here in mainland China during the Cultural Revolution. Why do I hold them differently in my mind than I do the Japanese invasion?

Mrs. Du is silent for a time but then she returns to her usual perky self and begins reading the poems inscribed around us.

She loves poetry. She first cornered me in the garden in front of my apartment saying, "Heathcliff, the administrator, promised that you would be my language partner." Since then we meet every Tuesday from 10:00 to 12:30 and chat about everything from bound feet to Russian literature. Mrs. Du is an English teacher and a leaner. I don't mean that she leans physically, but her personality, her very being seems to lean on me, the same way that China itself leans on me. Mrs. Du could probably talk me into anything, or lean me into anything. I'm not sure how I feel about that.

Mrs. Du is fifty-six years old, is married to a gentleman fairly high up in some form of government, and has been a card-carrying communist since she was a teenager and ran with the Red Guard. I haven't extracted too much information from her about her Red Guard exploits but she has managed, in her leaning persistency, to convince me that Chairman Mao is in fact an excellent poet. I didn't want to admit it at first but every time she comes over, she insists on reading me his poems from a book I picked up in the market.

"Chairman was not a perfect man but he had nice handwriting and wrote excellent poetry," she often says. Another saying she rhymes off is that "Chairman Mao was thirty percent bad, seventy percent good." In other words, he was worth the trouble he caused. It amazes me how she can use a blanket statement like that to justify just about anything. I've never met anyone like her. She's particularly content with her worldview and the shape of things here in China. And it's her generation, the former Red Guard, who are currently running the country.

I marvel at how she manages to exist here in China without questioning it—maybe the way a fish doesn't swim around questioning water. There's innocence and unbending strength in Mrs. Du. She's a symbol for the Chinese psyche—a paradox. Kind of like the police here in Nanjing: wearing their navy starched uniforms and white white gloves, sometimes they hold hands while walking down the streets, like children. But then I saw four of them in a confrontation with a street vending woman one night. She had a little kerosene stove for cooking food, and she and the four policemen were all tangled in a screaming mess fighting for it. It was a filthy little stove. They dragged her across the pavement as she clutched on to the thing. The policemen won the tug-of-war and threw the stove into the back of their pickup, along with about twenty other confiscated cooking devices. They drove away. The woman lay on the street weeping. I know that woman; I've bought steamed veggies and noodles from her and sat at her makeshift table and stools before. She feeds many people each night but she doesn't have a permit. The police drive around all night taking people's livelihoods away from them. But sometimes they just walk down the road holding hands.

All of this weighs on my mind as I sit with Mrs. Du and she, childlike, recites the poems all around us. Her voice is leaping and bowing through the rain as we wait for Cristina.

⚜

Considering how dense Chinese cities are, it's startling how quickly we pass from the gray six-story block apartments of Nanjing into tiny villages. Small white houses and black-tiled roofs huddle together by the side of the road overlooking the cultivated green fields that take up most of China's landscape in an attempt to feed the enormous population. In the gray city, today's low-hanging mist looked gloomy and sinister, but it seems well-placed over the fields, small ponds and between the houses. I feel like we're not only in the countryside but that we've taken a trip back in time.

Qi Xia Si is a subtle, dreamlike place. Tucked at the base of several small mountains, with a yellow gate that leads to a large square surrounded by more yellow walls, moon doors and fountains, it's so particularly Chinese it's almost too much, with the incense and the mist. Just entering the main courtyard, I feel the weight of the past week float off my shoulders and ease permeate me.

One of the principal Buddhist centers still active in China, Qi Xia Si is the home of the 1000 Buddha Caves—most of which were carved in the Tang and Song Dynasties, when China was at a cultural peak. I'm excited to see the statues and caves and feel my heart lighten at the thought that a place like this exists in China—imagine a whole mountain devoted to Buddha and bodhisattva caves, only twenty minutes outside of the city I'm living in!

I have the urge to walk alone through the grounds but Mrs. Du follows me everywhere, giving me history lessons in her booming voice and insisting that we each pay three yuan to have a chance to strike the enormous bell at the top of one of the temples. It's supposed to bring good luck or good fortune.

"Make a request and the Buddha will grant it," Mrs. Du says. I don't make a request—I'm not good at trading money for prayers. But the bell does make a beautiful sound as it resonates through the monastery.

"It doesn't seem Buddhist, paying to ring a bell and get a blessing," says Cristina, ringing the big bell. Cristina is an herbalist from Romania, doing her master's degree here in China. She was raised during the reign of Ceauşescu and loathes communism—a point she is rather vocal about. She's told me horror stories of having to line up for hours with her mother to buy the only food product for sale on a given day—be it dried shrimp or canned pineapples from communist-friendly countries such as Cuba. Her grandparents' family home was confiscated by the communists and her great uncle was killed by them.

"But, hey, in this place they call socialism 'social-ism with Chinese characteristics,' so why can't they have 'Buddhism with capitalistic characteristics'?" she says sardonically. "Hey, get beside that monk and I'll make a picture of you," Cristina looks suspiciously at the monk in his gray robes and woolen hat. "I hear that these temples are filled with army officers dressed as monks," she says. "I think he's an army spy."

It is difficult to understand the coexistence of religion and communism, but they do seem to coexist, at least superficially, here in China. Although the past fifty years have seen some serious damage to Chinese spirituality, there seems to be at least a feigned tolerance for religious sites, with newly rebuilt temples, churches and mosques. The government certainly has a monetary interest in religious practice and it often seems like tourism is the only reason temples are rebuilt and kept up. Maybe communism and religion have found a middle ground—commerce. I've heard that the CCP allows only atheists to become party members but here's Mrs. Du, a card-carrying communist buying into everything at the temple.

She's already purchased a two-foot-long stick of bright pink incense and made me take her picture while bowing to the four directions. Now she's taking her turn ringing the bell and posing for a photograph beside the monk. Irony creeps around the edges of my mind:

could this temple be merely a false-fronted amusement park that everyone, even good communists like Mrs. Du, is buying into? Is the government that organized and smart? The government has after all arrested the Panchen Lama recognized by the Dalai Lama and appointed its own. How do I know what is real? The ache of despondency fills me—I look around for an escape route.

Mrs. Du chats with the monk; I take my chance and sneak down the stairs and across the courtyard to a large meditation hall. It is set up for a service, with about fifty cushions on the floor and many monks filing through its doors. There are several lay practitioners standing at the back of the hall. I join them as the doors are closed behind me. Mrs. Du bangs on the door but the woman in charge opens it only a tiny bit and, to my great relief, tells her that she can't come in.

I'm not sure why I'm allowed to be privy to the ceremony—maybe because I'm a tourist, maybe because I have *yuanfen* "affinity" with Guan Yin, maybe because Guan Yin is taking pity on me and giving me a few minutes away from Mrs. Du's company and the reality of China. Regardless, I stand silent in the back of the tall temple as the monks prepare themselves. Two large plastic-tree-like glowing wheels with hundreds of golden Buddhas inset in them spin on either side of the large altar. And the statues on the altar are enormous—alienating rather than welcoming. There are a variety of Buddhas but no Guan Yin in sight; she's likely at the back, where they often have an altar for her. The whole place feels like a fun house at a fair rather than a meditation hall. Cristina's words echo in my mind: How do I know if monks are real?

They take their seats and a song begins—unintelligible insect chatter accompanied a by fish-shaped woodblock. A sloppy off-beat cymbal is introduced, followed by a high, clear bell. The chant reminds me of an engine having trouble turning over, unaware of any sense of time. Gradually, though, the voices begin to take the form of Chinese words—lots of *na, fo* and things like that. The gonging becomes more rhythmic and suddenly the monks, in unison, belt out, "Namo Amitabha."

My hair stands on end. The mantra has a deep, moving quality with a sense of longing. It doesn't matter that the statues are garish and ridiculously large and that a Christmas tree Buddha altar spins and glows in the darkness as the sound of the chanting permeates me.

I'm elated with a new sense of hope for me and for China as I push through the large wooden doors and meet with the bright gray light of day. Mrs. Du stands nearby. "You were in there for a long time. What were you doing? Don't you want to see the Buddha caves?"

I don't answer her. We walk through the courtyard toward the base of the mountain where Cristina sits.

In the first cave we encounter, the smashed faces and hands on Buddhas don't faze me—the carvings and statues just look old and worn out. It almost seems right that the faces are missing.

But by the third and fourth caves, when I notice how well kept the other parts of the Buddhas are—their gowns and the weapons on the guardian deities—the reality of what I'm looking at sets in. Sometime in the late 1960s or early '70s, people came to this mountain and destroyed the faces and hands of many of the statues only because someone told them to. Or they thought someone told them to. My guess is that they used hammers—the revolutionary tool of choice—to smash these symbols of the old culture and religion.

By the time we reach a small rest point, Cristina is on a fuming diatribe about the Great Proletarian Cultural Revolution. Thankfully, she is talking too quickly with her thick accent and swearing too much for Mrs. Du to understand her completely. But she gets the drift and responds, "Yes, when we were young, many people ruined many monuments. Most of them are sorry now. A wave passed over China in those years."

During the Cultural Revolution, Chairman Mao and his party decided that the people of China must do their best to rid society of the "Four Olds"—old culture, old ideas, old habits and old customs. This translated into a lot of destruction when interpreted by the masses. Places like Qi Xia Si and other religious sites were prime targets, but educated people—including poets and scholars—were targets as well. No facet of old society was spared, especially the elite or any member of a former government.

The Cultural Revolution lasted from 1967 to 1976 and saw hundreds of thousands of people persecuted and paraded through the streets having been charged with crimes that went against the principles of the revolution. An unofficial figure is that three million people were killed or died as a result of clashes during the Cultural Revolution. Universities were closed and people were sent into the country to labor camps and thought reformation camps. What is scariest to me is that language itself was perverted in those years to the point where to be considered a "compassionate" person would be deemed an insult and to be "destructive" a compliment.

Did Mrs. Du smash statues? Did she partake in rallies to prosecute the "capitalist dogs" and purify the country? It's hard to imagine her doing anything like that, she looks so cute and unassuming in her short pants and silk brocade jacket.

"What does sorry mean anyway? How does it feel?" says Cristina. "This communism is bullshit. It makes a stone in my heart. They ruined my country and they ruined your country."

"Many people felt that we should move forward and forget the old ways," Mrs. Du says walking toward the next cave. Cristina shakes her head. Mrs. Du continues, "The young people were very excited then. They believed that destroying old things was the way to the future." I stare at another smashed statue. During the Cultural Revolution everything was geared toward China's bright future. But when is the future? Here I am in the present looking at a broken past.

It's quiet on the mountain. Everything floats in a thin mist. I look at the space on the carvings where a bodhisattva's face once was. I touch the stone, feel the absence of face and begin to get dizzy. What I was thinking coming to China looking for Guan Yin?

"Look what they've done to Guan Yin!" I say to Cristina my ears ringing. I glare at Mrs. Du and want to give her an earful about what I think of her communist party and its jaded history and ask why she's so hateful toward the Japanese when her party did this to its own country-folk and cultural heritage.

But I don't. History feels too long and too deep to meddle with today. I want to be alone among the smashed statues, not only without my acquaintances, but without anyone. And that's nearly impossible. Tour groups spill all over the place with matching hats and megaphones; couples with dress shoes and fancy clothes pose for photos in front of faceless statues. I feel like I'm in a parallel universe. I came all the way to China and this is what I find.

I climb up to a lookout point away from the caves where some images are carved directly into the mountainside. I close my eyes to try and escape images for a while. There is a quiet pulsing to this place, with a slight breeze through the trees. This is the China I always dreamed of finding: a misty hilled landscape with caves full of Buddhas. What does it mean that most of their faces are smashed?

The Red Guard *believed* they were doing the right thing in destroying these artifacts. And here I am thirty years later believing they were wrong. Belief is far more destructive than ignorance. Ignorance is passive and festers with itself. Belief feigns certainty and tries to bully others into its worldview. Belief has nothing to do with truth. What about my own belief system? Is it narrow? Does it lull me with false comfort and security? What am I doing looking for an image in the People's Republic of China and then getting upset by reality?

Any look at Chinese history tells me that destruction of culture and religious sites is not a new phenomenon: during the Tang Dynasty, the very dynasty when these statues were first built, there was a Confucian revolt against the growing wealth and influence of the Buddhists and thousands of temples and monasteries were destroyed and hundreds of thousands of monks and nuns were ordered to return to being lay people.

That must have been horribly upsetting for those people. What is it about the distant past that turns massive upheaval into a mere statistic? Buddhism has risen and fallen many times throughout its history here in China and various schools have prospered and then shrunk. Nowadays we have mainly the Pure Land school, which promises salvation and merit by devotion, and Chan, which seeks to overthrow the rational mind through meditation and *gong an*—paradoxical questions such as, "What is your face before you were born?"

Sitting here at the site of the smashed Buddha heads, I've thought up my own *gong an*: "Is the smashed Buddha face still a Buddha?"

"Nin hao." A miniature woman with army shoes and a traditional blue coat approaches me. She has a bag full of something she's trying to sell. I pretend not to notice her. She sits beside me and places a small black plastic device in my hand. It looks like a miniature radio but it isn't a radio. When I turn it on it only plays one song. It's a recording of *Namo Guan Shi Yin Pusa*—Guan Yin's mantra sung by nuns. She can see that I like it and wants ten yuan. I don't even bother bargaining. I give her the money and turn on the player to full blast, elated to have Guan Yin's mantra ringing over the mountainside. My mood lifts and I keep the miniature radio playing as I stroll down the mountain to look for Mrs. Du and Cristina.

"Oh you have a radio," says Mrs. Du, grabbing at it. She turns it over and says, "Look, it says, 'Not For Sale.' I hope you didn't buy it. The peasants are deceiving; they get the religious materials and then sell them even though they are not supposed to be for sale."

It's true. The block gold printing on the back reads, "Not For Sale." In Chinese and English. I almost feel betrayed.

"I did buy it. I paid ten yuan for it off some lady up the mountain and it was worth the ten yuan," I say, though I'm not sure if I'm trying to convince myself or Mrs. Du that I wasn't ripped off.

"Too much," she says. "They should not be selling the Buddha."

Cristina scowls. "That's interesting if you consider that we had to pay twenty yuan to get into this temple complex. And three yuan to ring a bell. This place makes me crazy," she says. She's obviously had enough of Mrs. Du for the day. And my humor is wearing thin. The paradox that is China grates on me once more. It's time to go home.

We decide to take a cab instead of the bus. My treat. Mrs. Du sits in the front seat and converses with the driver. Cristina and I sit in the back seat. She looks out the window with her arms crossed and her face in an Eastern European frown. I look out my window at the countryside streaming past with my mini-radio defiantly playing on my lap.

Chapter 3

The Treachery of Hope (Lijiang and Leshan)
*Chinese New Year, an erhu concert, a Romanian poem,
and a visit to Xia Guan Yin Si*

I don't know the name of the raging blue lake just outside of Dali, where whitecaps rolled and echoed in the
mountains, but I was chilled by the time I made it to
the shelter of the small town. I shivered as I wandered
through the walled streets with tall gates leading to hidden courtyards.

I don't even remember the name of the town—a small
suburb of Dali. Most of the inhabitants were from the
Bai minority, dressed in red and white and going about
their daily lives without much contact with tourists. I
wandered through the lanes for a few minutes and then
stopped because I heard strangely sad music soaring
over the walls of one of the houses. The song held me
prisoner with its wailing strings and drum. I listened
for a long time as the notes rose and fell. Then the gate

opened and the music spilled out along with a procession, many of the people in white. It was a funeral. The song tugged at my heart as it disappeared down the lane and bent around the narrow corner. I made my way through the green fields and blue sky back to Dali.

There's a sense of height, brightness and space in Yunnan Province. And it's dry in winter—at least here on the plateau. The sky has been clear, cloudless blue for a couple of weeks, which might explain the name Yunnan—*south of the clouds*. Yunnan is also one of China's most diverse provinces, with at least twenty-five cultural minority groups dotted throughout the mountains and plains. It stretches as far north as Tibet and borders Myanmar, Thailand, Laos and Vietnam. At first glance, many of the groups here look like they belong to one of those South Asian countries rather than to China. But China has many faces and many races.

Most of the cultural minority groups here still have their own religions and traditional styles of dress, and the Naxi, descendants of Tibetan nomads in this region, still have their own pictorial language. During my hike through Tiger Leaping Gorge, I met a family who can still write it.

Tiger Leaping Gorge is one of the deepest in the world. It gets so narrow at one point that a tiger apparently leaped from one side to the other over the surging waters and enormous boulders. Members of the Naxi live staggered up the mountainside on one side of the gorge on small farms with terraced fields held up by rocks. I stayed with a Naxi family for a night during my hike. Their house was surrounded by a large gate and tall walls and was silent except for the lonely wind and clucking fowl.

Because the family belonged to a cultural minority, they were allowed to have more than one child. The daughter and son were both off from school because of the Spring Festival. They took me for a walk at dusk and we paused at the site of some graves. They were like miniature tombs with tiny doors and mounds of grass growing over them. They believed that the side of the mountain with the most spectacular view of the gorge and the range of sharp-toothed mountains was the most appropriate spot to bury ancestors. It's a tradition that's become impossible in eastern China, given the population in the cities.

We sat there as the sun dissolved and I hummed the teenagers the funeral song I'd heard in Dali. They hummed me a Naxi tune in reply. Since then, I've had a sort of amalgamation of laments in my head, dipping and soaring like the land here in Yunnan.

༄

After two weeks of touring around the province, I have finally made it to Lijiang, probably the most touristy city in Yunnan. Modern Lijiang is like any other small Chinese city with dusty streets, bike lane dividers and an enormous statue of Chairman Mao. But within modern Lijiang is the old town of Lijiang that has been preserved as a World Heritage Site and a kind of wonderland village where the Naxi people live "traditionally." And they do. Women in traditional Naxi blue and white, with children strapped to their backs in colorful embroidered cloths, carry fowl through the sea of black-roofed houses.

There are few private bathrooms in old Lijiang, and dozens of families share the communal ones, along with the tourists. The communal toilets are more like troughs than toilets. They're about a foot deep and about twenty feet long. Needless to say, they're not private at all. By mid-morning the troughs are filled with excrement and have to be swept out by someone in tall boots and then sprayed. This whole process saves on water because the old town just doesn't have the infrastructure to support everyone flushing a toilet. Most of the tourists hate the trough system at first but then grow used to it.

The old town is quiet and dark at night, so dark in parts I nearly got lost trying to find the guesthouse last night—there are few streetlights in the residential parts of the old town. But despite the appearance of traditional life, it feels precarious here for the cultural minorities. Judging by the rate of growth in China, the Naxi here in Lijiang seem to have two choices with the steady stream of tourists entering the region: to embrace the fact that their town is a tourist destination and sell their culture in organized shows and shops full of arts and crafts or to disappear.

Misgivings aside, Lijiang is a stunning village, with narrow granite streets, tiny canals, stone bridges and red lanterns in front of identical white houses in the basin of majestic mountains. It's the China from a storybook and an excellent place to relax and sightsee. Cristina and her husband, Razvan—my Romanian friends—have been here for two weeks relaxing.

Tonight is the eve of Spring Festival—the Chinese New Year. The old town bursts with firecrackers and there's an expectant buzz in the air. Most doorways have red poems written down either side, welcoming spring and fortune to the homes. Food is a big part of Chinese New Year and there are noodles and dumplings galore. The woman at the guesthouse has been feeding us incessantly and plying us with alcohol as we sit in her courtyard around a big table with blankets on our knees and a pot full of embers to keep our legs warm. She told me that it's bad luck to clean or wash on Chinese New Year because you end up washing your good luck away. That's why she hasn't been cleaning.

She's arranged for us to see a traditional Naxi concert with her friend, Miss Liu, who teaches *erhu*, a traditional musical instrument. The orchestra comprises many local Naxi musicians and will give us a taste of how great Chinese music is. But as usual with Cristina and Razvan, we're late.

"We are late. I told you we would be late, but no, you had to shop on the way!" Cristina says to Razvan. Although Spring Festival is traditionally a family time, all the shops are open because the town is full of tourists.

"I am not the one who had to paint my face before leaving the guesthouse," Razvan retorts. He slows down and smiles. Cristina and I slow as well. Razvan loves to argue. I've heard him start arguments in Romanian, Russian, English, Mandarin, French and Italian. It doesn't seem to matter who he's talking to, if Razvan doesn't agree, he'll start an argument. In fact, the first time I met him I got into an argument with him. I had just bought a new kite and was keen on flying it. I passed him on the way to the park outside of my apartment in Nanjing and he told me the wind was too soft for kite flying. Instead of flying the kite, we got into an argument about wind.

"Who made us more late: me looking at a painting or you painting your face?" Razvan asks Cristina.

"I'm not the one always buying fake gemstones!" she announces. Cristina takes off across the old granite square and Razvan, mildly embarrassed, follows her.

The problem is Razvan continually gets suckered into buying junk. Yesterday he spent a hundred yuan on a foot-tall "amethyst" cluster and marveled at what a great deal it was. I tried to convince him that it was a fake but he wouldn't listen. When we got back to the guesthouse he unwrapped it and wet his finger to wipe the dust from it. His finger turned purple from the dye. I told him to taste his "amethyst" and sure enough, it was made of salt.

The theatre is full when we arrive, but Miss Liu has saved seats for us on the balcony. At least fifty people are without seats, standing in little pockets and corners and behind poles. The musicians tune their instruments, cellular phones ring, and everyone seems to be smoking. Cristina introduces me to Miss Liu and tells me that she has been playing *erhu* since she was a child and has a great knowledge of Chinese music and a great love of all music. Although Miss Liu is a traditional music instructor, she is anything but traditional. She smokes Marlboro cigarettes, has dyed red streaks in her hair, and is wearing a slinky shirt.

The orchestra begins. The instruments twang, wiggle and bend the notes. I sit beside Miss Liu and she translates the song titles and talks about the importance of the *erhu*. The *erhu* apparently came from Mongolia and was originally only a folk instrument. It wasn't until the Qing Dynasty that its merits were appreciated among the upper classes and it was used in court and in operas. The bow of the *erhu* is fixed between its two intertwined strings and a small sound box made of snakeskin makes the sound resonate. *Erhu* is one of the instruments responsible for the sounds of deep longing in Chinese music.

"The *erhu* makes my eyes water with its lilting melodies and dipping sadness," I say to Miss Liu after a couple of songs.

"This is the point of music," she says "to play on the heart strings and speak what the tongue cannot speak. This song is about spring."

We listen to the song about spring and it reminds me of some time or some place that I've forgotten. "If it's about spring, why does the music sound so sad?" I ask.

"Because those who play music are sad." She points to the musicians in the band, many of whom are older members of the Naxi minority group. She explains that they are losing their musical traditions and that many of them were persecuted during the Cultural Revolution and had to hide their instruments underground in the fields, so they have reason to be sad.

"But eventually," she says, "music is neither sad nor not sad—it's the listeners who decide. It is through their ears that the song passes. Is it not true that sometimes very sad songs make us happy and very happy songs make us sad? It is not the fault of the *erhu*." She lets out a large cloud of smoke.

I begin to wonder if my ears might be tuned wrong because it doesn't seem to matter what is played on the *erhu*—it makes me sad. In fact, everything I've heard in Yunnan, from the funeral tune to the Naxi children in their school uniforms, has had a hint of sadness in it. I try explaining this to Miss Liu after the show. She suggests we do an experiment to see whether my ears are tuned wrong. I agree.

Outside the theatre the spring festival celebration is in full swing. Children run everywhere with lighters in one hand and firecrackers in the other. Sparklers and piles of paper money burn on the street. Miss Liu pauses by a bench and rummages through her bag for some plum liquor. She tells me to have a swig and then listen to the fireworks.

I listen. She asks if the fireworks made me sad.
"No."

She concludes that my ears are not tuned wrong—if they were, the fireworks would also make me sad. But because the *erhu* music makes me sad and never happy, it is clear that I listen to the *erhu* improperly, and I don't understand Chinese music or spring, because they should make me at least "happy-sad." She lights a cigarette and tells me to drink more plum liquor. She says that many poets and musicians and painters celebrate the beauty of the plum blossom in the spring and that drinking it might help me understand. I take another swig.

"I think that you might be wrong, Miss Liu," Razvan says, gearing up for an argument. "The *erhu* is meant to sound sad when it plays songs about Spring. Just as poems about spring make us sad. It is the sadness of expecting something, and of knowing that it will never come, or if it does come, it won't last—like spring, and then summer. Romania is filled with such sadness." He stands upright and presents a poem, first in Romanian, then he and Cristina translate it into English:

> *You came and stayed with me for a time.*
> *I still feel how weary you were.*
> *When we discussed the melting of cold days*
> *And the treachery of hope.*

"The treachery of hope?" I ask. "And sadness about spring? You think I'm sad about spring?"

"Everyone knows that spring is equally as sad or more sad than fall or winter. But you might be sad about the treachery of hope, not about spring," says Razvan.

Cristina nods and tells me that she thinks it's a political poem about the end of communism rather than a poem about spring but that Razvan's sentiment may be right. We should all beware of the treachery of hope.

Miss Liu and Razvan enter a discussion about the treachery of hope in Mandarin. I hear the word *xi wang* several times—meaning *hope*. But other than that, I don't understand what they say.

"Now hold this sparkle-bomb and I will make a picture of you," Cristina says to me.

I hold the sparkler beside my face and try to smile for the picture. But the treachery of hope haunts me. It haunts me as the sparkler spits and fizzes its amber light down to a metallic char. It haunts me as I walk through the dark streets beside Miss Liu. I wonder what hopeful illusion I'm in. The first thing that comes to mind is Guan Yin. The next stop on my trip is Sichuan, where I will visit a small temple called Xia Guan Yin Si. One of my main reasons for coming to China was in search of Guan Yin's house, so when I heard that there was a little temple on a hill dedicated to her, I knew I had to go to Sichuan to see it.

In dreams and visualizations I often see Guan Yin's house on a hill, surrounded by bamboo, overlooking a body of water. Part of me hopes that the temple is her home—but what if it isn't?

I tell Miss Liu my dilemma. She pauses for a minute and takes a long chug of plum wine. "Most music resolves and doesn't leave the listener hanging in a sad note—but sometimes the overall mood is sadness. On the other hand, sometimes there's an unresolved note at the end of a song but the overall feeling is uplifting. So I think that no matter if you find Guan Yin's house or not, you will feel both sad and happy because that's the way things are."

We walk on. Miss Liu and I drink more plum liquor and enjoy the festivities. She sings and hums as she walks and tries to teach me a folk song in Mandarin. The lyrics are about being nothing but a tiny piece of grass blowing in the breeze, but in that smallness not being sad.

Razvan and Cristina keep falling behind, stopping at shops and arguing about whether or not to buy souvenirs. We eventually lose them in the lanes.

Miss Liu and I sit on a bench by one of the canals; the water flows quickly, gurgles and spits at our feet. I think about Guan Yin. Guan Yin is known as the bodhisattva who listens to sounds. Her name, "Guan Shi Yin," literally translates as "observe world sound." She is also known as the "Regarder of Cries." It is her compassionate way to bear witness to the suffering of the world through listening to her devotees' pleas. She's even known as being born from a tear that the Buddha shed for the sadness of the world. If anyone knows about sad sounds, it's Guan Yin.

Somewhere near midnight I ask Miss Liu whether she thinks that Guan Yin gets sad when she listens to the *erhu*. She pauses for a moment and announces, "Guan Yin probably gets sad when she listens to the *erhu*, but she doesn't dwell on the sadness. That is the difference between you and Guan Yin: she hears the music, and the sadness, but doesn't drown. You do. That is why you are a human and Guan Yin is *pusa*! Let's go to see the fireworks."

In ancient China, there was apparently a beast called the Nian who ate people. Everyone was afraid of the monster and thought that he could sneak into houses and kill families. At some point they found out that the Nian was afraid of loud noises and the color red. So everyone wears red and blasts away the bad spirits with firecrackers on New Year's Eve. The word *nian* also means *year* in Chinese. I wonder if the myth about the Nian was a roundabout way of saying that time is going to get us all in the end.

We walk out of the old town toward the main street. It looks like a war zone. I can see why firecrackers are banned in some cities. Gray smoke clouds the streetlights, and red scraps of paper and ashes blow in the breeze. Children hold miniature cannons blasting colors and noise. Men on big tricycles, who by day might sell vegetables, ride up the street selling piles of fireworks.

The clock strikes midnight and people stand facing forward like artillery. Some carry bags full of fireworks. They are mainly men with cigarettes in one hand and every possible combination of fireworks in the other. Some of the explosions create pretty colors against the sky, but mainly they tear the night with noise. Miss Liu joins in and blasts several whistling pink bombs across the street while I stand in a corner, my ears plugged.

The fireworks die down and the streets empty. Pieces of burnt fireworks blow in the breeze, a thin dust hangs in the air. Miss Liu and I walk through the new town. She hums quietly. We reach the large statue of Chairman Mao and she yells, "Chairman Mao, nin hao!" and then continues singing her song.

The bus trip from Lijiang to Sichuan province was nauseating. I was crammed into the window seat beside a woman and her child. The child's father sat across the aisle beside the grandmother. They were a poor family and probably uneducated. But they were kind. When they first entered the bus, the child needed to pee. And although we hadn't pulled out of the station yet, instead of taking the child outside to pee on the road like most children do (they have built in holes in their pants for such occasions), the father had the idea of having the child pee in a paper bag.

Both father and mother made "ssssss" sounds and placed the bag between the boy's legs; on cue, he peed. It didn't take more than a few seconds for the bag to moisten. But the child kept peeing. He peed and peed until the bag was saturated. Then the father, with a look of dismay, tried to run the bag through the bus to the door. Everyone watched him scramble as it dripped and puddled along the aisle and finally broke apart, dumping the remaining contents just beside the driver's chair.

Things calmed down once the bus began moving, and the child sat happily on his mother's lap with his feet on my knee as we pulled out of the station.

The sun burned and the sky was thin blue en route to Sichuan. I was dizzy from altitude as I looked over terraced fields, staggered up the mountainside like green bricks, from the depths of the narrow valleys to soaring peaks. The little white bus climbed passes that were too high for comfort and more than once I feared we would roll off a cliff.

The woman beside me was friendly and offered me sunflower seeds, smiling at me as we ascended. I ate the seeds and smiled back.

And then she started screaming at me, but I couldn't understand a word she said. It was like a wall of noise, accented with high-pitched screeches. I felt like I was being assaulted. The child started crying and I was cornered between the screaming lady, her kicking child, spilled sunflower seeds, and the window.

Then I looked out the window. My view had changed. The woman in front of me was vomiting and yellowish bile raced across the lower portion of my window. I closed the top portion of the window before she vomited again. I nearly vomited myself. The woman beside me nearly vomited too. Everything was moist and smelled like pee and bile.

At that point I remembered something that Razvan said to me the other day. He said that eventually you stop fighting China because you know that you can't win. So I tried to just accept my situation. I closed my eyes so as not to look at the vomit on the window and tried to ignore the pee and bile smells. All was well, except for the invasion of my mind by the tape of cheesy love songs blaring through the bus speakers. Like most Chinese buses, that one was equipped with a scratchy stereo to play tapes at the driver's discretion. That driver liked cheesy love songs, and he liked them loud. There were about five songs on each side of the cassette, all whiny with guitar solos and sax. As time went on, I grew agitated and had visions of myself climbing to the front of the bus and flinging the tape out the window.

I tried to relax and think of Guan Yin. It's said that she achieved enlightenment through the sense of sound. She penetrated the essence of sound and knew that all sounds were the same. I reasoned that she'd be able to listen to that tape of cheesy love songs without getting worked up, just like she can listen to sad *erhu* music without getting sad. So I kept my eyes closed and tried to hear the essence of sound. But after another round of the tape, even the driver grew tired of the love songs and turned the music off. I was saved by default.

By late afternoon, the bus entered a silent buzzing and most of the passengers slept. I continued watching terraced fields and tiny houses. I watched them reach from the bottom of every valley to the dizzying heights of each mountain. I watched terraced fields and tiny houses until it was pitch black and then dreamed of terraced fields and tiny houses.

My first meal in Leshan is Sichuan hot pot with two Canadians from Fredericton—Leslie and David. Leslie is an outdoorsy woman with a sense of adventure, here for a couple of weeks visiting David, who has been studying Mandarin in Hangzhou for a semester. David is a lanky musician who plays trumpet and guitar. They're backpacking in the southwest of China and were robbed at knifepoint in Kunming a couple of days ago by a man wielding a large rusty machete. Understandably, they have a world-weary air about them and are suspicious of being ripped off again.

A wok boils in front of us with a spicy broth and there's a plate full of vegetables to be cooked. But the food tastes metallic it's so spicy—none of us can eat the vegetables once they've been in the broth. And none of us dare eat uncooked vegetables, so we sit here in culinary limbo. After a minute or so someone forgets how spicy the hot pot is and attempts another go. I've done this several times and keep frying my taste buds. The restaurant is full of other tourists—all Chinese—and they all seem quite able to stomach the hot pots—or they were wise enough to ask for mild versions.

I explain my journey to David and Leslie and they listen. They're excited to go to the site of the Guan Yin Temple with me because they want to see Dafo (the largest Buddha in the world) and he's in the same park as the temple. Dafo was built in the eighth century and took several generations to complete. He is 227 feet tall and in the likeness of Maitraya—the Buddha of the future.

The idea for constructing a large Buddha came from a monk called Haitong. Haitong believed that the image of the Buddha would calm the waters of the turbulent rivers in Leshan. And it did: the stones that were chipped away from the cliff while constructing the Buddha were placed into the river and in time redirected the current!

Neither Leslie nor David can quite understand why I believe that Guan Yin's house actually exists here in China, but both are sympathetic to the idea of a journey. I tell them that I, too, can't quite understand why I believe that Guan Yin's house actually exists in China, but that hasn't prevented me from traveling to Sichuan.

Leslie asks me what I will do if the temple isn't Guan Yin's house.

"I'll just keep looking," I say.

The hot pot bubbles its spicy brew in front of us, and I feel the beginnings of doubt creep into my mind again. I remember the Romanian poem about the "treachery of hope" and try to push it from my consciousness.

We desert the rest of the hot pot and walk out of the restaurant onto the overcast street to hail a cab. We tour through the city and take in the sites. Like many smaller towns in China, Leshan has a gray, post-communist hue over it and its people. Old men and women, still dressed in their revolutionary suits, sit in large groups playing mahjong or other games in public areas. The air is damp from rain last night, but the day soft and calm.

"I don't like this taxi driver," Leslie says after a time.

"Yeah, it feels like we've done a circle," says David. "Maybe he doesn't know where he's going."

The man eventually drops us off in front of a large ornate gate. David asks him if this is the gate to Dafo, the large Buddha, and the man smiles.

Several makeshift booths stand in front of the gate selling statues, pictures, and incense. The vendors all call to us, waving trinkets. Again, I have mixed feelings about my contribution to the commercialized tourism of religious sites here in China.

A man with a box of baby chicks, all dyed ridiculously bright colors of pink, blue and green, tries to sell me one. I have the urge to buy them all and set them free. I imagine them hopping around on the dirty, wet streets in their vibrant colors, brightening the day. They wouldn't last the morning. I wonder how Guan Yin's house could be just inside these gates and if these little chicks are getting dyed on her doorstep.

We pay the entrance fee and enter the large park. An enormous reclining Buddha is carved into the side of the mountain, and several large statues adorn the park—but many have been built recently. The large Buddha was built 1300 years ago, but some of these look like they were made last year. I grow suspicious.

We follow the signs that say Dafo, getting drawn deeper and deeper into the park. We pass an enormous staircase leading to a large sitting Buddha in a cave and several other large statues, but none of them are the large Buddha we've seen in pictures. We walk and walk, following signs, and eventually come to a gate. Another gate, with another entrance fee.

"We've been duped," I say.

"I knew I didn't like that taxi driver," says Leslie. "Forty yuan more? I'm not paying it."

"But we've come all this way," I say. But Leslie and David have already been ripped off enough this week.

David argues with the guards, but they're not at all interested in our story. They insist that there are two separate parks and we've already seen one. If we want to see the other, we have to pay again.

"The taxi driver took us to the wrong gate," says David. "They know that foreigners will pay twice to get in. But not me." He crosses his arms. Leslie crosses her arms. They sit down among the bamboo and say that they'll wait for me.

I walk over to the guards, look at their official gray suits and hats, give one of them forty yuan and say, "Cao ni." Both of their faces drop. David and Leslie laugh.

"Good pronunciation!" David says. But I immediately feel bad for swearing at the guards: it's probably not their fault that we're being charged again—they're just doing their jobs. I feel all hot and prickly and can hear my heart beating in my ears as I stroll past them into the park down a narrow lane surrounded by bamboo and other foliage. All the signs lead to the 227-foot Buddha, but I want to see Guan Yin's temple first.

I come to a clearing with couple of buildings and what looks like a dining area. I enter one door and meet a small round-faced monk.

"Guan Yin Si zai nar?" I ask. He stares at me, and then directs me out the door and up a path. A sign, in Chinese characters, reads "Xia Guan Yin Si" (Lower Guan Yin Temple). The sign points up the hill. I jog up, excited to visit Guan Yin's own temple. It's quiet. A river stirs through the bamboo—this seems like a perfect spot for her to live. A place where that she can listen to the world's sounds without distraction.

I reach the top of the hill. There's no one around. I can read the name "Xia Guan Yin Si" written in Chinese characters above the three identical doors that stand open on the temple. But it seems empty. I see right through the building where the bamboo sways in the breeze.

I feel dizzy. My flesh crawls as I cross the threshold. The temple is bare. Cement floor. Nothing on the walls, no altar, no lights.

The treachery of hope. No Guan Yin. Empty.

A woman in a worker's outfit appears. "Mei you Guan Yin," she says. She spits on the floor. I walk out the back door and cry because it's so perfect. The woman calls out to me, but I don't understand what she's saying. I smile sadly at her and she turns away. I am alone behind the empty Guan Yin temple. The bamboo rustles in the breeze.

Chapter 4

✢

Guan Yin Peak (Anhui)
*A visit to Yellow Mountain and Mr. Grappa,
the Chinese hand painters and the practice of qigong*

The streets of Tang Kou were flooded when we pulled in,
rain half a foot deep rolling down the hill. The man at
the guesthouse told me that it's been raining for a week.
That's why the rivers are gushing, that's why the trees
and bamboo have that phosphorescent breathing hue
to them, and that's why there are so few travelers—relatively speaking.

I knew it was going to clear up though. I knew it
the other night as I slept on the bunk in the train, the
windows wide open with the rain pattering in and that
hot, hot tropical night smell as we moved further south
in Anhui province. I knew it would rain until we arrived, and then it would clear up so we could see the
majestic Yellow Mountain—Huang Shan. It cleared up
this morning and we climbed.

There's nothing yellow about Yellow Mountain; it's all lush greens and jagged gray spires with steep, twisted pathways carved out of the rock. Huang Shan's name came from Huang Di, the Yellow Emperor, the reputed ancestor of the Chinese people who commissioned magic pills for immortality to be made here.

But what I especially like about Huang Shan is that it has no overt religious or political significance. I climbed Taishan last year and it was a wonderful ascent, but the entire mountainside was riddled with political poems and legends, while the other, more spiritual mountains in China are riddled with trinket shops and faux prayer rooms filled with dirty little deities demanding money for prayers.

Huang Shan, unique among mountains in China, with its dripping craggy rocks, spindly pines and serpentine clouds, is the home of the artists. Situated in southeastern Anhui province, it is about nine hours south of Nanjing by train—and is immensely popular with Chinese tourists.

Matt and I have been ascending for about three hours; I can feel it in my calves. Matt is a traditional Chinese medicine doctor, practicing here in China for a year. He's always thinking about the five elements and *qi* and carries acupuncture needles everywhere with him. In the winter he walked around like an old Chinese lady with a plaid scarf tied around his kidneys to "keep warm."

He has long-fingered, thin, steady hands and plays the guitar. Matt is also an avid surfer back in Australia. And he and his brother and cousins have a habit of posing naked, in surfing postures, at famous sites around the world—like on the Great Wall of China or in front of the Eiffel Tower or Big Ben. I've photographed Matt naked on Hunnan Lu in Nanjing and now on Huang Shan's spires, completely naked and crouched over as if he's surfing on the drifting clouds and craggy peaks.

Other than laughing about the naked photos, we've walked mainly in silence, occasionally exclaiming at the beauty around us. About fifteen minutes ago we rounded a bend and saw a twisty staircase leading up to a soaring spire. Although we knew that we could go around it, we decided to climb up and take in the view.

"Welcome to Cloud Viewing Peak! I don't know if that's the proper name, but it's the name I've given it. I thought it sounded terribly Chinese. Ha!" The man, probably Italian, is drunk, sitting on a wall of rock with his back to a sheer drop of several hundred meters. He wears a white cotton button-up, a tanned brown vest and an Indiana Jones hat. His three friends seem equally drunk and all look like they're about to teeter off the side of the mountain.

"Have a drink. You've made it. Have a seat. It's not the top, but it's better than the top because there's grappa," he proclaims.

Matt and I sit. I take a plastic cup of grappa and watch the two Chinese painters seated beside the drunk Italians.

"Ahh, the painters. You know it's an old art form. I think only a handful of schools still teach it. Finger painting. Black and white. Do you see the fingerprints in the ink? Isn't it wonderful? These fellows are good," says the man I've decided to call Mr. Grappa.

The two painters have large pieces of white paper and palettes of black ink. Using only their fingers they capture the landscape—wispy clouds, dizzying heights, grotesque rocks and trees. There's something beautifully human and flawed about the fingerprints in the crevices, in the foliage on the paper.

"Art and writing are capsules where we attempt to fossilize the today as it slips away from us, too beautiful to catch and yet we still try," muses Mr. Grappa. He refills my plastic cup.

"Are you a painter?" Matt asks Mr. Grappa.

"I used to be. But now I just talk about painting. Isn't that terrible? Ha! Are you a painter?" he asks Matt. And we all laugh; I don't know why, but it seems like a funny question. I explain the purpose of our trip: to see Huang Shan and to find Guan Yin peak—the best place to do *qigong* and gather *qi*, according to my *qigong* teacher. Gathering *qi* is something like gathering "energy" or "life force," in that *qi* can mean the very stuff that life is made of—both matter and consciousness. But although *qi* is in all things, *qigong* practitioners insist that there are some places where it's more plentiful. And Huang Shan is one of them—specifically the valley of Guan Yin peak.

At the mention of Guan Yin peak, the painter on the left has looked up and smiled. He's been looking up and smiling for a couple of minutes now.

I finish my second cup of grappa and realize that if we don't get out of here soon, Mr. Grappa will pour me another drink. I stand up to leave and the painter calls to me, "When you get to Guan Yin peak, close your eyes. You will feel her." I smile and understand. Things between Guan Yin and I have taken on a more ethereal approach since I traveled all the way to Sichuan and found her temple empty. I try to give my cup back to Mr. Grappa.

"Interesting that a visual artist would tell us to close our eyes," I say.

"Why do you think that is?" says Mr. Grappa. "Do you think that visual art is only about seeing? Do you think that poetry is about seeing? Huang Shan is a wonderful place. I always come here, every time I'm in China. Today I am with my brother and sister and her husband. They think it is pretty, but they are missing why I love it. I come here because here I love life, because I love where I am. I am here—I am on Huang

Shan! Poets and painters and kings have been coming here for thousands of years. This is the most wonderful place!" He pours more grappa in my glass so I can salute Huang Shan once more.

"Look at the color. Look at the amber. Feel these smooth stones? See these twisted rocks and trees? Hear the wind. Can you smell the clouds?"

Mr. Grappa's sister, brother and brother-in-law all laugh. "He thinks he is a philosopher," says Mr. Grappa's sister.

But I agree with Mr. Grappa. The present moment might be all that there is. Too bad that the only place he can surrender to it is on Huang Shan, but at least he's found it somewhere.

"I know what you mean," I say and hand him back the plastic cup. I follow Matt down the steep rock steps to the pathway that leads to the summit of the mountain.

"See you on the top!" Mr. Grappa calls after us.

For a long time afterward I can hear Mr. Grappa's voice as we walk over the rock bridges sifting through the clouds until we meet another great stone staircase winding up between two tight peaks with an enormous boulder balanced overhead.

There is a saying in Chinese about Huang Shan: If you visit the five famous Chinese mountains, you never need visit another mountain. If you visit Huang Shan, you don't need to visit the five famous mountains. I think that might be true. I begin to feel a little like Mr. Grappa. Maybe I'll buy myself a cottage on Huang Shan.

We round a bend and run right into a pack of delivery men. Climbing delivery men. They climb from the bottom of the mountain to the top and back down again every day with bulky, weighty loads of food, carpentry supplies, and garbage. There are six of them in a row, snaking up the next steep pathway, their calves the size of thighs. Each day, up 8000 stairs: How do they do it? In their post-communist blue pants and flat-soled camouflage shoes with no arch support—how do they do it?

My earlier musings about being in the present on Huang Shan take on a different dimension. There's Mr. Grappa with his Indiana Jones costume drinking on a beautiful spire and here are these guys, heads down, sweat pouring off them as they carry cases of water and beer up 8000 steps to the hotels.

Who is appreciating what about Huang Shan? Matt and I watch them round the bend above us out of sight.

"Do you think those guys think about the future as they walk up the mountain, or do you think their minds are present?" I ask.

"Well, they climb the mountain every day, so it wouldn't do much good thinking about the future."

"It's like Sisyphus!" I yell over the narrow valley between sheer rock faces. My voice echoes back at me.

We emerge from the narrow pathway beneath the suspended boulder and stumble onto a noodle vendor: four yuan for the noodles in a packaged bowl and another four yuan for boiled water. That's a good trick. These will be the most expensive noodles I've eaten in China. We sit overlooking another valley along side hundreds of "lover's locks" that people have attached to the guard chain. You can buy lover's locks at various stalls on the way up, have your names carved in them, and then affix the locks to your favorite precipice as a testament to your love—or something like that.

The noodles are the packaged MSG kind inside a disposable bowl. My flavor is beef. Matt's is chicken. They've been percolating or whatever it is that noodles do for long enough; they're getting cold. If you avoid the flavor-fat packet you can avoid the meat. We put it on anyway; Matt thinks we need some protein.

After stopping on several precipices where Matt stripped naked and had me photograph him in a surfing posture with clouds wisping by, we finally reached the summit. As soon as we entered the little village of restaurants and hostels I remembered how populated China is. People were milling about everywhere, having dinner, posing for photos, checking into guesthouses—most of which were full.

Matt and I finally found a guesthouse that was more like a prison, all cement floors and walls and one naked lightbulb dangling from the center of the ten-bed dorms. Lucky for us there was room. We had to stay in separate same-sex dorms but the other beds were empty in both rooms so we thought we'd struck gold—surely no one else would arrive at such a late hour.

Just as we were about to leave to watch the rest of the sunset, a convoy of tourists marched toward the guesthouse, all wearing bright red hats with the name of the tour company on them, while their leader, wearing the same red hat but also a matching red jacket, brandishing a red flag in one hand and swinging a megaphone in the other, directed them down the narrow lane and then to their rooms—our rooms! The tour leader has told them all to wake up at four a.m. to catch the sunrise. Both Matt and I know from past experience that the likelihood of a Chinese tour group going to sleep is almost none. They settled into their rooms—our rooms—and immediately pulled out beer and cards, cigarettes and nibbles and sat down for an all-nighter.

Consequently, we sit on a rocky precipice, having our own all-nighter, minus the smoking, drinking, card playing and snacks. We've been here for about two hours, watching the sun set behind jagged peaks and the moon rise from behind jagged peaks. The moon is half-full tonight. It floats like a boat in a sea of blue and frothy white clouds above us.

I love the moon. And the moon is an important symbol in China. It's affiliated with *yin*, in the theory of *yin* and *yang*. There's a moon festival once a year in the autumn when the entire country goes outside to watch the moon and eat moon cakes. There's even a Guan Yin called "Water Moon Guan Yin" and Guan Yin visualizations where she stands on a crescent moon and dissolves into the void. Whenever the moon is out, I have the feeling that Guan Yin is close.

"Hey, do you think that you can feel the moon if you close your eyes the same way that the artist said I'd feel Guan Yin if I close my eyes on Guan Yin peak?" I ask Matt.

"Why don't you try?" he says.

I stand and assume a *qigong* posture on the cliff beneath the moon. In *qigong*, *waiguan* is the practice of stilling the mind by concentrating on an external object such as the moon. *Neiguan* is the practice of stilling the mind by concentrating internally on the body. Although most of us have the habit of looking outward for understanding, my *qigong* teacher says that if I seek the origin of nature, a good place to start looking is my own mind. I've been practicing for only a few months but *qigong* does bring a subtlety to perception similar to sitting meditation.

Qigong employs *dong* (movement) with *jing* (stillness). Some accounts say it has been practiced in China since 10th century BCE. There are written explorations of its health benefits by the Yellow Emperor in his famous *Huang Di Nei Jing*. And after it became clear that *waidanshu*—the "magic pills for immortality" that had been commissioned by various leaders—were actually made of gold and arsenic and were poisoning people and making them crazy, members of the ruling class turned their energies to cultivating themselves internally through *qigong* rather than looking for outside agency to lengthen life. *Neidanshu*, or inner cultivation, works with the breath and visualization, attempting to transform *jing* (body essence) into *qi* (breath or life force) and *qi* into *shen* (mind functioning or consciousness) and *shen* in turn into *xu* (void).

The Chinese tell a story about a girl taming an ox that works on similar principles. The ox symbolizes primordial nature. At first the girl has a terrible time trying to calm the ox, then she eventually trains it and no longer has to keep it tied up. She can sit beside the ox playing her flute and it won't run away. Over time the ox turns from brown to white, almost transparent, and wanders among clouds and the moon, and the girl sits and contemplates in the moonlight. Eventually the ox disappears and the girl is there witnessing absence.

Then the girl disappears and there's only the moon illuminating the void.

Matt and I stand on the edge of the cliff. I close my eyes and try to feel the *qi* of Huang Shan and the moon.

"Well. Can you feel the moon?" he asks after a time.

"I feel a lot of things," I respond. My voice sounds like it's coming from a distant valley.

"I see pulsing lights in my mind's eye," he says.

"Me too!"

There are indeed flashing lights—two flashlights brandished by a lady from my room in the guesthouse and the manager. They shine the lights directly in our faces like we're being interrogated by the police and explain that we can't stay outside, although I don't understand why. We explain that we can't sleep inside because of the smoke and noise. They say we must come inside at once anyway.

It was near impossible to sleep with all the card games, drinking and smoking in the guesthouse. Everything settled down by about three a.m., and by four a.m. the tour leader was in the hallway with his megaphone waking everyone up to see the sunrise.

Scurrying through the darkness, people pile on steep rocks, moving like floppy monsters in the dark. We climb and the day gradually lightens, or maybe that's my eyes adjusting to the darkness. It's velvety out still. We have to hop a fence to get to the sunrise peak. I often find myself in this situation in China—in a large mob doing something that I wouldn't normally do. I wonder if this is what group mind is: when I stop thinking as an individual and just do what everyone else is doing. I can't tell if we're all going to just flop our way off the side of the mountain like a pack of lemmings. I decide that the people with megaphones—of which there are at least four—have likely been here before and won't lead their tour groups off a cliff. They beckon us forward in the darkness.

We finally settle on a perch and wait for the sun. First the echo of its light from beneath the clouds paints the morning soft pink until finally—flaming red—the orb burns into view, illuminating various peaks and a sea of clouds so thick and fluffy I want to walk on them. As the day continues to bleed in, I realize how many people there are perched on this precipice—some of them chewing away at salted meats and tofu snacks, many dressed in matching tour uniforms and many others wearing rented army-green jackets for warmth. Their voices grow louder as the day grows.

Matt and I become quiet, closing our eyes so as not to attract attention to ourselves. But it doesn't work. Suddenly they're upon us—the yellow-colored tour group—asking for us to pose for photographs. They separate us so that we can be twice as effective. I get to hold the tour group leader's flag, while Matt wears a bright yellow tour hat. The bold link arms with me, and the bolder put their arms around my waist and shoulders like we've known each other for years, as their friends snap photos of us against the red sky.

"Let's get out of here," Matt yells to me from the edge of the cliff. And we scramble away before anyone else discovers us.

Descending, we soon find a misty solitude in the clouds that swirl around us, periodically parting to give a view of the sharp peaks and dripping trees. We have two maps: one glossy cartoon of the mountain with various peaks, including Guan Yin peak, illustrated; the other, a map drawn in ink by my *qigong* teacher, with only a few peaks, including specific directions for where to turn to get to Guan Yin peak.

"I think it's a way off still," says Matt, looking at the noodle vendor we've just encountered. The noodle vendor agrees that Guan Yin peak is a way off. "Maybe we should have some breakfast."

It's a repeat of yesterday's noodle adventure, only this time they're charging five yuan for the boiled water. We slurp shrouded in clouds.

"I hope that Guan Yin peak is visible when we get there."

"Isn't the point to feel the *qi* rather than see the peak?" asks Matt.

"I'd still like to see her," I admit.

We continue our decent—descending is always more difficult on the legs. But I can't complain, especially when we meet another group of delivery men with heavy loads of wood on their backs. We stand aside to let them pass.

"Why don't they use the cable car for delivering things?" I ask.

"Maybe these guys would be out of a job if they did. I've seen far more useless jobs here in China—but we have to keep people employed."

I've also seen far more ludicrous jobs in China, like that of the man who stands on a small red podium beside the entrance to the university. His job is to ensure that cyclists dismount and walk over the threshold while entering or exiting. People on motorcycles and scooters don't have to dismount; in fact, it seems like they speed up while passing the gate. Still, the man stands there all day making sure that every cyclist dismounts. But no one actually does. Everyone has a technique of swinging one leg over and balancing on one pedal while crossing the threshold. Somehow this is acceptable, although it's clearly more dangerous.

Is this what socialism reduces to: invented jobs to keep people busy? It makes me think about the myth of Sisyphus again, how it's not only applicable to someone in a tiring physical situation like these gentleman or with a mind-numbing task of making people getting off of bicycles—but how it sums up life itself.

"Aren't we all ceaselessly toiling away at life—trying to find meaning, impart meaning? Isn't that the basis of all religion and belief: to try and make sense of our labor and pains, to try and make it worthwhile because through these trials we're getting somewhere?" I ask Matt.

"Oh don't get all existential. You're almost there."

"But that's the point. Why go 'there'? Why do I strive to leap past futility and pain and wait for future promised lands? Why can't I find Guan Yin peak right here!" I stop and sit on a lump of rocks. I look back up the steps we just came down—thousands of steps carved out of stone.

Matt pulls out the water and we have a drink. He closes his eyes. Sisyphus—the myth holds a clue—it has liberation inherent in it. But not liberation from—liberation in. Sisyphus had nothing to look forward to except his rock rolling back down the mountain after he rolls it up, day after day. He had to find his liberation in the limitation of his task, in the present moment, because it wasn't ever going to come through linear time running out. Guan Yin is similar. The *Heart Sutra* says that she realized that matter isn't different from void and so realized that there's nowhere to go—no heaven to look forward to; in that way she is free to keep manifesting as her compassionate self in this world.

"It's the idea of future, the idea of finding something somewhere other than now that keeps me bound as I roll my rock through life..." I say.

"Do you want to continue?" Matt laughs.

"Sure, but I'm not getting all worked up about finding anything specific."

Still, I become excited when we finally reach the turn onto the path leading to Guan Yin peak. We wind through the trees, past some pavilions where people pause for lunch. Luckily, the trail is off the main path enough that many of the tourists don't use it. It winds and winds, rounding through a little wood and then down into a lookout point carved out of the rock. It's narrow, the stairs are steep, but once we make it to the end, it feels like we are in the heart of Huang Shan. There's a bowl of rocks surrounding us for 360 degrees—a private mountain range within the mountain range—and the lookout is built on a narrow pathway of rock leading to the top of a weathered hoodoo. It gives me vertigo.

"This is stunning," Matt says. "I feel a little dizzy. I'm going to go up to that little ledge in the trees we just passed and lay down."

"What?"

"I'm going to have a nap."

"You come all the way to Guan Yin peak and then fall asleep!" I say following him up to the trees.

"Something's come over me. I'm tired—I want to sleep," he says, laying down on the dried pine needles. I sit on a small rock and feel the hint of sleep wash over me tickling my neck and head.

"Have a good sleep then," I say. His breathing deepens and he blends in with the stillness of the valley. Directly across from us stands a vista of sharp rocks against the sky that look like bodhisattvas—likely where the name Guan Yin peak comes from.

I leave my bag beside Matt and climb back down the staircase to the hoodoo, the circle of peaks surrounding me. A silence has settled on the morning. A solitary silence that grows louder. Maybe it's exhaustion from being awake all night or maybe it's the space I feel. The cliffs and soaring rocks appear to come closer and then recede.

I take an open stance in *qigong* and think about Guan Yin. My teacher always says that Guan Yin is a great *qigong* practitioner—that she's tuned into the nature of things. I close my eyes and listen to my breath and the sound of saliva in my throat.

I stand still for several minutes until I can feel the *qi*, see the *qi* and hear the *qi* mingling with the sound of the breeze. My body begins to move slowly with the *qi* until I am part of the landscape.

I open my eyes and everything seems to be coming apart. The mountains, the trees, the sky; my hands are not as solid as usual, and much brighter. I turn around. Matt sits on the steps behind me.

"Everything sparkles," he says softly. And it does.

Chapter 5

❧

The Statue Crisis (Gansu)
*Xiahe's Labrang monastery, Om Mani Padme Hum
and sneaking into Tibet*

Western China is dusty. There's nothing romantic about the poverty on the edges of the cities as it manifests in great numbers of gray-clothed people milling about, waiting for I don't know what. And bathtub tile buildings with ill-fitted windows—a white one beside a pale blue one beside a soft salmon one, with pointy buttresses on one and roman arches on the next. The buildings look like they don't quite know what they are or where they are.

We've been rattling westward for days—spent about a night on the train from Nanjing to Xian where we visited the Terra Cotta Soldiers, stone faced, lined up in their airplane hanger guarding Emperor Qin. Then we took another overnight train to Lanzhou. We were going to continue west and visit Dunhuang, the home of the Buddhist caves along the Silk Road. But we flipped a coin and decided that I've seen enough Buddhist sites for the time being and that we should visit a Tibetan settlement instead. And so we're heading south, safely away from statues and Buddhist carvings.

Like most Chinese buses, this one has a driver and a ticket collector, who sits at the front and when we pass people on the road asks them where they're going, determines a fare and collects the cash. The ticket collectors are usually congenial people who must have a lot of patience to ride around on Chinese buses all day. But the ticket collector on this bus is possibly the meanest man I've ever seen. He just looks angry. His face is permanently red and he keeps threatening people with his fist. I tried bargaining with him and gave up very quickly. He's already thrown two people off the bus and has punched a man at the front who doesn't have enough money to pay for his whole trip. Sadly, the poor man has two children with him. They sit quietly and watch their father get roughed up. He takes the abuse and keeps looking down, seemingly so they'll let him stay on the bus longer.

"I'd like to throw that awful man off the bus," Hanne says. Hanne is an even-tempered physiotherapist from Norway who believes wholeheartedly in fairness, equality, and Lutheran principles. She also plays underwater rugby and practices kung fu and is probably the only person on the bus who could take the angry ticket collector.

"I guess we could pay for the poor man," I say.

But before we work up the courage to stumble through the entire bus to the front, the man, his large striped plastic bag, and his two children are pitched off the bus onto the dusty road. We pull away.

"What a horrible world," says Hanne after a time. She closes her eyes and leans against the window.

On a map of China, I imagine our bus is almost dead center right now, which is interesting, considering how many Tibetans there are on board. I always imagined Tibetans cloistered up on the Tibetan plateau, but it seems that they've lived out here in the green mountains and plains for centuries.

We're on our way to Xiahe—the southwestern corner of Gansu province. Xiahe is the home of Labrang monastery belonging to the Gelukpa (Yellow Hat) Sect. The monastery was founded in 1709 and many Tibetans still live in the surrounding mountains.

The countryside is carved with rivers, dipping through green hills and mountains. We clatter further south, streaming past solo travelers and entire families standing by the side of the road in the middle of nowhere with big burlap bags, dusty wind-blown hair and tired eyes.

Speaking of eyes, I try not to turn my head to meet the two staring at me on my right. The owner of the eyes is so close I can hear her breathing, with her head turned ninety degrees, staring at me. This has been going on for quite some time. It's not that I'm afraid of the woman—well, I'm partially afraid—but I don't feel like engaging in or miming a conversation.

What is fear? What is so attractive about it? Fear must be a close relative of desire because I begin to confuse my fear with desire—the desire to turn toward her, engage with those staring eyes. I face her. Her mouth: the largest big-teethed, gold-rimmed slow smile. And her eyes: large flashing eyes. I suddenly understand where the artists who paint Tibetan deities get their inspiration—from Tibetan women! Her features are so intense they are otherworldly. I half-smile back and she smiles again. She points to my rings and then to her own. Tibetans seem to love jewelry, their hair entwined with lapis, turquoise and bright red coral. She points to my eyes and then to the sky. She takes off a gold ring and hands it to me. I take off a silver ring and hand it to her. Her fingers are thicker than mine.

She reaches into her jacket—a traditional coat with one of the arms off the shoulder and tied behind her back—and pulls out a plastic bag filled with some crunchy treats. The coat is a great place to store things.

Hanne wakes up and directs my attention to the monks in front of us. They've been clowning around for hours.

"He keeps grabbing the other monk's hand and putting it on his crotch," she gasps.

"What?" I sneak a peek between the seats and there's something kinky happening under the cassocks in front of us.

"Oh gosh, this isn't good," says Hanne.

"Maybe they aren't monks…" I say.

"Of course they're monks!"

I don't have time to worry about the monks as the woman beside me pulls an enormous knife out of her jacket. I can't for the life of me figure out how it fit in there comfortably. She holds it up for me to see. I smile, hoping I'm not designated dinner. But slowly she replaces it into her jacket along with the snacks and whatever else she keeps in there. This is the Wild West. Whatever happened to the cute Hello-Kitty-wearing Chinese boys and girls in the Chinese cities?

"They're practically on top of each other!" cries Hanne.

"Quiet, or they'll hear you."

"But they aren't supposed to do such things. Aren't monks supposed to be celibate?"

"Yeah, well maybe they have a loose understanding of celibacy here."

"You're terrible," she says.

"I'm serious."

"I know. That's why I said that you're terrible."

Suddenly, another monk, sitting a row in front of the two promiscuous monks, turns around and they separate themselves.

"So it's a secret affair," I say.

"Of course it's a secret—they're monks!" says Hanne. But I feel sorry for them having to live a double life.

Having become accustomed to a country filled with small-boned, pale Han Chinese, walking into a town full of Tibetans is like a trip to another planet. They're tall, ruddy with those permanently rosy cheeks, cowboy hats and cool sunglasses made from polished stones. There's a tavern of sorts across the dried up river bed from our guesthouse, where they stand beside dusty motorcycles—chrome horses—possessing a disarming air of freedom and strength.

The guesthouse is called Green Tara and is set behind a store filled with many colorful woolen materials for clothing and sundry for travelers: soap, toothpaste, beer, and the like. The owner tells us to heed the evening curfew and that this town, although friendly to travelers, is no place to be wandering around after hours in the dark. Xiahe is essentially a strip of shops with gray garage doors rolled up that will likely roll down at night and become deserted.

We check in and settle into a little room. I like the guesthouse specifically because of its name: Green Tara. Green Tara is the youthful and compassionate Tibetan Buddhist deity known for her playfulness in helping those in need. She's usually depicted in the "half lotus" position with one leg stretched out, symbolizing her willingness to leap to people's aid (different from White Tara, who takes a more contemplative approach with both legs crossed). Some people confuse Tara with Guan Yin because they're both compassionate. But in Tibet, Guan Yin is called Chenrezig and is depicted as male, often with eleven heads and a thousand arms, with an eye in each palm symbolizing his infinite perceptive powers and compassionate wisdom. Depictions of Chenrezig always make me a little unsettled—like they're revealing a side of Guan Yin that I'm not quite ready to witness.

All night long I heard them spinning in the darkness: 2500 prayer wheels that surround Labrang monastery, each about five feet tall that. I loved the sound—creaky and airy—and I loved the thought of pilgrims out there in the night, circumambulating, spinning prayers into the mountains and across the world.

At first light I went onto the roof to listen and watched the pilgrims in their spinning. Most Tibetan Buddhist prayer wheels have Guan Yin (Chenrezig) mantra inscribed on them: *Om Mani Pay May Hung* (Tibetan) or *Om Mani Padme Hum* (Sanskrit). Prayer wheels are created in the belief that spinning the wheel has the same affect as saying a prayer. The vibration of the written prayer spins out through the ethers the same way the uttered word does.

Om Mani Padme Hum translates to something like "Oh thou jeweled lotus!" and is said to be the subtle mind of Guan Yin. Whoever recites it develops her compassionate heart, and those who penetrate the meaning of the mantra will become her. That is the promise of mantra.

All of this feels rather hypothetical as I exit the guesthouse and join the pilgrims in their spinning. I walk and spin, and the more I spin, the slower my thoughts become. The prayer wheels are all painted wonderfully rich Tibetan burgundy, bright blues, and yellows.

One important thing I notice about such large prayer wheels is the law of inertia: it's a lot easier to spin a wheel that's already in motion than to set one spinning that has stopped. Maybe that's why the pilgrims take turns spinning them all night.

I follow the pilgrims in their determined pace, their long matted hair filled with bones, stones, and coral.

I don't look directly at each wheel or I get lost in the spinning and the colors blur in my eyes. The pilgrims murmur *Om Mani Padme Hum*.

About fifteen minutes into the circuit, several pilgrims have overtaken me, although I'm going as fast as I can without breaking into a run. An older woman comes up beside me and grabs my arm, pulls me out of my walking meditation and says, "Holy, holy!"

She pulls a ring off her finger, slips it onto mine and says *Om Mani Padme Hum*. The ring spins—it's like a mini-prayer wheel on my finger with the mantra engraved on the spinning part. Before I have a chance to say thank you she takes off down the row swishing prayer wheels as she goes. I follow her, whispering *Om Mani Padme Hum* and watching her weathered brown hands, agile on the wheels. She's an accomplished spinner.

We finish the circuit together and she walks, without slowing her pace, not unlike a mountain goat, up a steep pathway until she disappears behind the mountain. She doesn't turn back.

Does she live up there? How does she sustain herself? How do any of these pilgrims sustain themselves? They seem almost unscathed by the Chinese occupation of this area—but that's likely only a superficial impression. There's probably some dark tale about how the Chinese half of this town was settled. In fact, there's still a clear division between the Chinese and Tibetan parts made apparent by electricity at night: the Chinese part of town is illuminated; the Tibetan part is not.

I meet up with Hanne for breakfast in a little café near the guesthouse and realize that I'm freezing.

"Man, it's cold here—it's July and I'm freezing," I complain.

"I told you that you should have brought a sweater," she chides. "You pride yourself on traveling light and then travel too light." She sips her tea in her nice warm Norwegian sweater.

"Wo hen lung," I say to the waitress.

"She has a fine sweater," says Hanne. "Why don't you ask her where she got it. We could get you one."

I ask the waitress, and she asks why I want to know. I tell her that I'm foolish and cold and need a sweater. She laughs and walks away.

A Western man in the next booth turns around. "Why are you speaking Chinese to a Tibetan?" he asks in that angry traveling tone that some people possess.

"Well, she doesn't speak English, and I don't speak Tibetan, but we both speak some Mandarin," I say.

"You are colonizing through language—she doesn't want to speak Mandarin," he says. He's kneeling on his chair and hanging over the back of Hanne's booth.

"She seemed quite happy to speak to me," I say to the man.

"And where are you from?" Hanne pipes up. She turns and faces the man.

"Oregon."

"What do you have to say about colonizing? Your government was in China, along with several other countries, trying to colonize here long before the Chinese invaded Tibet!"

He opens his mouth to speak again and Hanne bursts in, "Don't speak to me unless you speak Norwegian. Don't colonize me with your filthy English." She proceeds to rattle off a long, lilting Norwegian paragraph. The man, speechless, and bright red, turns back to his breakfast.

"There isn't much worse than a self-righteous traveler who complains about a disappearing culture while eating PANCAKES off an English menu, with numbers to point at for the non-English speaking waitress, in a Tibetan town in the middle of China," says Hanne, loud enough for everyone in the café to hear.

The waitress returns with our congee and then takes off her sweater and gives it to me.

"Oh no," I say.

"Song gei ni," she insists and walks away. Hanne and I eat our congee in our warm sweaters and I think about the openness of the two Tibetan women I've met in the past hour and the man, eating pancakes, who thinks I'm a colonizer. I do agree, and Hanne probably does too, that language is an effective way to take over a place, but it's too easy for Westerners to come to China and find things wrong with the country.

As we get up to leave, I take off my favorite ring and hand it to the waitress. She tries to give it back, telling me it's worth too much. I insist that she take it and walk away; it just feels right.

By the time I enter the main halls of the lamasery, I'm dizzy from all the statues. Little bodhisattvas in cupboards, towering bodhisattvas that must have been assembled inside the rooms they're so big, all watching from meditation poses between bejeweled stupas. Part of me wants to hop onto the altars and disappear into them for good, another part wants to run to the fields and escape their staring eyes.

"They are rather creepy. Why do they possibly need so many statues?" asks Hanne starring at a large rendition of Manjushri, the Wisdom Buddha. But even I have to admit there is an excess of statues in the lamasery. And there is something eerie about the otherworldliness and sheer size of them lined up in one enormous hall after another.

"Is this what I came to China in pursuit of? Images?" I ask aloud. The statues don't answer. They just stare through me into infinite silence.

"Are you coming?" Hanne calls from the end of the hall. I keep falling behind the tour group.

We enter a damp, dark room. On the altars sit yak butter sculptures of bodhisattvas, lamas and small temples leftover from the Tibetan New Year festival in February. As soon as we pass the threshold into the room, it's clear that the yak butter is rancid—the pungent air makes the German couple gag.

"Oh, what a smell," says Hanne. "Why would anyone want to worship in here?" She passes out the door quickly, along with the rest of the tour group.

I linger. On closer inspection, I see that the butter would be an easy material in which to carve out detailed images. That said, the seasons have changed and the sculptures have gone off and melted in parts. But I'm curious as to why they chose a material that would decompose so quickly—or maybe that's the point. Tibetan Tantra seems to fancy the idea of emptiness. What better way to exemplify it than a statue of the Buddha or Guan Yin dissolving?

There's a lovely rendition of a bodhisattva that I'm drawn to. I walk across the room to take a closer look. There's noise coming from behind it.

I peek around the side of the sculpture right into the eyes of a large brown rat! I jump back and it continues to chew its way around the base of the bodhisattva, unaffected by my presence, wiggling its long tail in prayer.

Hanne comes back into the room, "What are you doing? The tour's over; we have to leave."

"Look at that rat," I say, filled with a strange kind of excitement. Some part of me likes the idea of the rat eating the bodhisattva.

"Oh gosh! This is disgusting. And there's more," she points further down the hall where more rats munch on rancid butter Buddhas. "Let's get out of here before one of them bites us."

We move quickly down the dark hallway away from the stench of rotting butter and into the light of day.

The rancid butter Buddhas reminded me of a dream I had a little while ago in which I found myself in a garden filled with statues of the Buddha and Guan Yin. The statues kept getting closer and closer to me and then parts of them started falling off, nearly hitting me in the process. Eventually they all dissolved and I was just standing in emptiness. I woke in a cold sweat.

The shop is a statue collector's dream—old wooden carved sitting Guan Yins, ancient oxidizing bronze Buddhas, decapitated Guan Yin heads likely stolen from some pillaged temple, pocket-sized Guan Yins, all facing forward watching.

A Han woman in a dusty gray suit and green army shoes stands among a fine array of antiques and beckons me to come and see. At the back of the store stands a bronze Guan Yin about two feet tall with delicate features, flowing gowns, and the Buddha on her crown. I like her immediately. I figure the statue is expensive, but I want to know how expensive. I ask the woman.

"Yi bai (100 yuan)," she replies.

"Yi wan (10,000 yuan)?" I ask, thinking I must have misheard her.

She laughs and repeats, "Yi bai."

One hundred yuan isn't even twenty bucks. My first thought is that the statue must be cursed; otherwise the woman would never sell it at such a price. My second thought is that Guan Yin must want me to have the statue. This is a more agreeable thought, so I go with it. I try to lift the statue, but it's so heavy I can barely move it.

"I'm buying this statue," I say to Hanne.

"Are you mad?"

"No. I'm buying it right now for a hundred yuan. Now help me lift it."

"But, Sarah, you cannot carry that to Tibet; it's too heavy. It will never fit in your bag. You simply cannot take it."

"But I can't leave Guan Yin here all alone," I say, getting dizzy again and hearing my voice echo in my head.

"What are you talking about—it's a statue and it's probably done quite well without you for over a hundred years. You're acting like a crazy person," she scowls.

"I'm not crazy. It's Guan Yin and if Guan Yin can't go then I'll stay with her," I announce.

"And what will you be staying with?" Hanne asks and walks away. "Hurry up or we'll miss the bus."

It's hard to describe how Hanne's words fall on me. I stand in the dusty shop with the shopkeeper smiling and a statue too heavy to lift. It's clear that my understanding and connection to Guan Yin is changing. It needs to change and will continue to change with or without my cooperation. I leave the shop without the statue and make my way to the bus stop.

The nine-hour bus ride from Xiahe to Xinning passes through many diverse landscapes, from plains to the greenest rolling hills to steep mountains to semi-desert, and is witness to nomadic groups living in tents, Tibetans, and many Muslim Chinese. We drove through entire towns with white Muslim hats on top of Chinese faces and out the other side through blankets of green grass where young Tibetan men flew past on motorcycles, tearing up the earth and with long hair blowing in the breeze. We're still in "China," but it's clear that China is a relatively new country and its borders reach into places it wasn't invited.

Muslims have lived in this area for more than six hundred years. I have a Uyghur Muslim friend whose family comes from Xinning. He's told me tales about the Manchu rule of China during the Qing Dynasty (1644–1911) when an anti-Muslim sentiment flourished and the government used their armies to repress Muslim regions and their culture. He's also complained that the cultural genocide for Muslims during the Cultural Revolution was as bad as what happened in Tibet and asked me why most Westerners haven't even heard about it. There are approximately twenty million Muslims in China today.

Although the Chinese government recognizes its hundred-plus cultural minority groups, many people from those groups, my friend included, have a difficult time getting an education, mainly because they're poor. But even if they are educated, it's difficult to climb the administrative ladder because most cultural minorities have religious beliefs and the CCP likes its members to be atheist. Racism and bigotry are surprisingly prevalent in China.

The bus stop in Xinning was a tough place. We tried to buy a bus ticket to Lhasa, but the ticket lady said we couldn't get one unless we had a permit to enter Tibet, which was about 1200 yuan. The ticket would be another

1000 on top of that. The whole thing sounded fishy, so I asked a few Chinese travelers how much their ticket for the ride cost: 270 yuan.

I took another lap around the bus station and met up with a rather fat man with an entourage of surly looking men. He had a large wad of cash in his hand, so I knew that he did business. I asked him if he could get me to Lhasa without a permit. He said, "1000 yuan." I told him that I was with a friend, how about both for 1500? He agreed. He gave us enough time to buy some unleavened bread from an Uyghur street vendor and then hurried us into the back of his "friend's" bus.

We're on the top bunks along the back of the bus crammed beside two Han Chinese and a Tibetan woman. None of us are able to sit upright because the roof is too low. The expected trip length is fifty-two hours and we're not allowed to open the blinds because if we're caught we'll be kicked off the bus and the driver will be fined 10,000 yuan per foreigner.

We've reached a happy medium: I keep the blinds closed except for a little peek hole so I can see the scenery. Hanne insists on having middle bunk because she doesn't need to see out the window.

Within the past three hours I've seen one capsized bus and another capsized truck. They didn't look like serious accidents, just inconvenient. The roads are narrow and twisty. Qinghai means "green sea" and the province has certainly earned its name—the grass blows and rolls like green waves as we carve our way into the heart of the continent.

Lying down on a bus is terribly relaxing. I know that this ride is supposed to be taxing and horrible, but it's such a wonderful feeling to travel horizontally across the land, drifting in and out of sleep. The falling night has a dream-like quality to it. The earth and sky pulse, and I feel an openness and expanse growing in me as the landscape flattens.

"God is in nature," Hanne says somewhere along the shores of Lake Qinghai as we skirt it in the dark. The green plains have turned to sand, and I can see the curve of the earth on the horizon. The night sky is crisp, clear with the moon casting her blueness over everything. Stars sit on the edge of the lake, on the edge of the desert—the firmament burns.

"I have a guardian angel, you know. And my guardian angel knows yours. I could tell you had one the first time I met you," Hanne announces in the dark. I picture Guan Yin and some Norse Christian angel convening somewhere among clouds and scented mists. I laugh out loud.

"I'm serious!" she exclaims.

"I know," I say, not quite sure what I'm laughing about.

We fall asleep somewhere in the blue night. I dream of Guan Yin. She is standing before me on the plains with a full moon overhead. I walk toward her. I'm so excited to see her. She opens her arms as if to embrace me. But her arms continue to open, wider and wider, until she holds the entire earth within them. I am one of countless things floating in her arms. Her arms continue to expand until she holds the entire galaxy, then the entire universe. Nothing exists outside of her. Nothing.

We awake in Golmud—possibly the most desolate city on the planet. We eat noodles at a greasy little restaurant on a dusty patch of earth. Around the corner is a stinky public toilet that's guarded by a grubby man and three large chained dogs that bark incessantly. The scene is nauseating but we force ourselves to eat.

After we finish, the driver refuses to let us back onto the bus. Instead, we are ushered into a tinted windowed car with a Tibetan woman and a Chinese driver. I sit in the back between the woman and Hanne.

The woman speaks some Mandarin. She tells us not to worry and hands us two musty old Tibetan coats.

Hanne is questioning everything because our bags are still on the bus and we're driving through the countryside. The woman puts a balaclava on Hanne to cover her blond hair and tells her to be quiet.

She gives me a cowboy hat and then puts her arm around me and says, "Pretend you're sleeping—pretend you're old and wise."

The day is so bright it seems foolish to pretend that I'm old and sleeping. And Hanne, in a balaclava in the middle of July, is even more ludicrous. But one look at Hanne's blond hair or my blue eyes would give us away, so we go along with the ploy.

The woman keeps patting me like I'm a pet. And my back gets sore from sloping over onto her for so long. She smells like yak butter and smoke—like one of the temples in a lamasery.

We drive and drive and my mind creeps toward what might happen, the police opening the doors and taking us out and charging us. But I pull it back and pretend that I'm old and wise. My face is moist from the dampness of my breath, all huddled in the arms of yak-butter lady. I spin my new ring out of nervousness and imagine its little prayers permeating the car.

Finally we arrive at the checkpoint and the yak-butter lady rearranges my hat so that it hangs down over my face. She hugs me even tighter and pets my head much harder than you would ever pet a sleeping person.

I have no idea what Hanne is doing—she's perfectly still beside me. I close my eyes the way children do, as if not being able to see will make me invisible. The driver speaks to the guards but I can't make out what they're saying. I realize I'm not breathing and take a deep breath. Yak-butter lady does as well. We keep breathing, my head against her chest.

The car begins to move again and she loosens her grip on me. She pulls the balaclava off Hanne and heaves a sigh of relief. We drive for a while longer until we enter some low mountains. We round a dusty, rocky mountain bend—everything the color of dried mud—a lunar landscape.

The car stops. Yak-butter lady tells us to get out. We take off our coats and hand them back to her. She says goodbye and hops into the front seat beside the driver and they begin to pull away. I suddenly feel like I have Stockholm syndrome—I don't want them to leave. I bang on the side of the car.

The yak-butter lady rolls down the window and I ask her what we're supposed to do. "Deng (wait)," she says and hands me two cigarettes and a pack of matches. She smiles a big grin and says something in Tibetan and then rolls up the window. They drive away.

"I feel like I'm on the moon," I say.

"This is not good. What if the bus never comes? What if they were pretending that this is the right way?

Our bags! There isn't even any water to drink!" yells Hanne.

We stroll a little way off the road near a large boulder to hide behind in case the next vehicle isn't our bus. Hanne sits down and I lean against the enormous rock overlooking a dusty gorge that must have once held water. It's oddly beautiful. I strike a match and light a cigarette. I'm spinning off the first drag. We wait.

Chapter 6

༄

The Statue and the Statue Maker (Tibet)
A visit to Yeshe Tsogyel's nunnery,
a bus full of farting nuns and no-fixation

Underwater. I hear a steady beat. I think it's my heart. I surface and I gaze up a steep green valley full of prayer flags draped liberally across it at various angles, converging in great tangles of color and mantra. I wonder if the sun ever makes it into the tiny caves above me where nuns have meditated for hundreds of years and where the Dakinis supposedly fly.

Tibet is one of those places that is simply not warm enough for me—even in broad daylight in the middle of summer. I've been cold since we arrived here, until now. Now I've entered the heart of the country: I float, pale, silent in a hot spring in Tidrum: Yeshe Tsogyel's nunnery.

Yeshe Tsogyel is probably the most famous Tibetan yogini. Some say that she was originally Chinese and although she asked her parents to become a nun, she was sold to the Tibetan king because of her beauty. She attempted escape and was captured by a few hundred soldiers who flogged her and returned her to the king.

Luckily, the king of Tibet was a congenial man and wanted to understand the Buddhist teachings so that he could achieve enlightenment in one lifetime without having to renounce his senses and pleasures. So he invited the great Indian guru Padmasambhava to the palace to teach him Tantra. The king offered Padmasambhava anything he wanted in exchange for the teachings, and Padmasambhava asked for Yeshe Tsogyel because he knew that she would be a good student.

The two of them ran off to some caves and he taught her the Tantric way. After he gave her a series of initiations, she realized that every situation is a "play of empty being" and understood that pleasure and pain were identical. This didn't happen until she'd had tribes of demons from Nepal, India and Tibet try to scare her from her practice and handsome young demons tempt her. She even managed to convert a bunch of rapists into disciples because she was so in touch with her Buddha nature.

She went on to serve anyone who needed her assistance, from healing the sick to becoming the wife of a leper. She was free from all concepts. She served Tibet throughout her life, and she and Padmasambhava hid their teachings in *terma*—treasure chests scattered throughout the country, to be found when people were in need of the truth. She warned that in the future, the country and the teachings would be corrupt and that people should remember the *Om Mani Padme Hum* mantra.

Her predictions may be true. Many would agree that the government now running Tibet—the Chinese government—has corrupted it. But as she requested, the six-syllable mantra *Om Mani Padme Hum* spins on prayer wheels, flutters in the breeze on all the prayer flags, and is carved into *mani* stones throughout the country, giving the place a fairy-like quality despite the hardships that the Tibetan people have endured.

Maybe it's the stories of sages such as Yeshe Tsogyel in my head, or maybe it's the vibrant colors of the country, but nothing feels particularly real here in Tibet—especially when I consider the four nuns in burgundy robes, peeking over the railing at Hanne and me in the hot spring. They giggle and recruit others to come and see us.

"What are they looking at?" asks Hanne.

"Our naked bodies?"

"Oh gosh."

We do seem rather pale and green against the dark rocks in the middle of nowhere in the middle of Tibet.

"Why are they so fascinated with us?"

"I don't know. If we can spend all this time and money coming here to peer into their culture, why can't they take a peek at us? And better they look at us than the Dakinis eat us, Hanne. Yeshe Tsogyel was a Dakini—one of the female spirits who haunt these mountains! I've heard of people offering body parts to Dakinis—they'd make quick work of us this morning if they spotted us. They mustn't notice our offerings," I exclaim.

"Eating body parts? What are you talking about now? I don't want to hear any more of your gory stories—why don't you say something pleasant?" She swims off.

Hanne is still shaken from the sky burial we witnessed yesterday while hiking here. It burns in my mind too. In attempting to reach the road into this narrow valley, we took what we thought was a shortcut up the mountain above the Drigung monastery. Partway up we looked skyward to see about forty Griffon vultures circling.

After reaching the top of the low-grassed rolling ridge of the mountain, we hiked in the direction of the nunnery and stumbled onto a sky burial site. It was clear what the site was: not because of the hundreds of colorful prayer flags that adorned the fence around it or the large tower of incense burning toward the sky, but because of the mass of carrion birds tearing at what was left of a body that had been chopped up on the stone slab. Once the vultures finished eating, the ravens took a chance and picked up the dregs.

We sat outside the enclosure, transfixed with swirls of incense wafting around us. We stared for a long time at the large stone slab and the absence of the body.

Sky burials are the norm in Tibet, maybe because the earth is too hard to break in winter months. Watching the ceremony yesterday was similar to witnessing the burning *ghats* in India, but more optimistic—maybe because of the spaciousness of the setting. Sure, birds had just eaten a human being, but it was a beautiful view, and there's something natural about being eaten.

I've been thinking about it a lot since yesterday, first because of the actual ceremony that we witnessed, but also because of where we were heading—Yeshe Tsogyel's nunnery. Dakinis sometimes hang around charnel grounds and meditate on the transitory nature of all things, and this land somehow radiates that vibration. But I have been talking about guts and sinews a lot, and Hanne has reached her limit with my mortal musings.

Sinking below the water level, I blow bubbles in the silent heat and try to think of something pleasant. But I don't know what pleasant is any more. Maybe "pleasant" is a concept—just like "unpleasant" is a concept. I know that I spend most of my time seeking out and reaffirming pleasant things and avoiding unpleasant things.

But what am I missing in the meantime? Life? Tantric philosophy states that we can't solve life's problems by aversion or attraction: both extremes have to be given up. Maybe that's why the Tantrikas hang around charnel grounds—abolishing both hope and fear.

The bus that comes to the nunnery twice a week is leaving today and will take us back to Lhasa. Below the tangle of prayer flags and steep green hills, Hanne and I pile into the bus with about thirty nuns. The nuns are catching a ride to the end of the valley, where they will do some roadwork. Several of them hold rakes and shovels. They're a jovial bunch with wide eyes and smiles. There's so many of them that once the seats are filled, the rest stand single file in the aisle, giggling with shovels and rakes clanking.

The driver and ticket collector pile in, the music is cranked and we're off. The nuns in the aisle scream and laugh as we bump and twist on the narrow road. It's taking most of their energy to keep from toppling onto those of us who sit. Their laughter is infectious and Hanne and I soon join them. This lasts a couple of minutes until Hanne's face changes.

"Oh gosh, there's a terrible smell. I think the nuns are all farting," she says.

I'm by the window and can't smell anything unpleasant. The laughing continues and Hanne grows progressively more uncomfortable.

"Don't have an aversion, Hanne. It's just a smell," I pontificate.

"You're crazy," she says.

I only smell diesel from the bus and the fresh breeze from the window.

"Oh gosh. I think I'm going to vomit," she says. She heaves and covers her face. I think back to the meals we've been fed the past couple of days: the only food they had at the restaurant by the nunnery was cabbage and eggs. The thought of it makes me a little queasy. Most of the food in Tibet has made me a little queasy.

And then the smell reaches me. It's like we're on a portable toilet that's overflowing. I want to laugh but have to stick my head right out of the window for fear that I will vomit.

The bus stops and I hope that the farting nuns are getting off. But we pause only long enough for the driver to switch seats with the money-collecting lady. I can't figure out why they've traded jobs except maybe the woman was getting nauseous from the stench back here.

"Do you think someone has shat themselves?"

"I don't know. I've never smelled anything like it," I breathe shallowly and try to keep the smell out of my lungs.

And we're off again. Hanne and I are hanging out the window and the burgundy mass of nuns are farting down the gorge. The money-collecting lady is a terrible driver—she keeps accelerating and then slamming on the brakes. Everyone is jostled. I reach into my pocket for my Pocket Guan Yin; I always hold onto her when situations get bizarre.

"We don't need that thing, we need nose plugs!" Hanne says looking at Pocket Guan Yin.

I clutch her tiny form anyway. Saying her name is supposed to be enough to save you from all sorts of perils. I figure that holding onto her has a similar effect. We come out of a bend and are on a straight stretch beside the river where the gorge opens onto a flat valley.

The ticket-collecting-lady-turned-driver accelerates for about ten seconds before launching us off the road into a ditch. We're stuck. I can hear the wheels spinning, but it's no use. We're on a forty-five degree angle and half of the wheels are in the air. The two bus drivers crawl out, argue in Mandarin, the nuns giggle and walk off toward the roadwork they're supposed to do, and I find a grassy knoll to sit on and get my bearings.

The Tibetan plateau is truly the roof of the world. It's flat, with mountains peeking out from the plain, though not very high—because the plateau is already over 3500 meters high. The sky is only a short way overhead and it isn't a dome like it was on the plains. I feel like I can touch it. The grass is ultra-green, with wildflowers. But the grass is different than it was in Qinghai—not so long and voluptuous; summer isn't a very long season here and growth is strained. There's something approaching desolation about the whole place, something haunting, almost sad.

Up above us on the mountainside I see the Griffon vultures circling like they did yesterday. I guess there's another sky burial today. A woman at the guesthouse by the nunnery told us that people travel hundreds of kilometers to get a sky burial at this site—it's supposedly a blessed place.

A man rides out of nowhere on a fine horse and laughs at the drivers. He looks at me, then up at the birds, smiles broadly and then smacks his lips.

Hanne sits beside me and looks at Pocket Guan Yin. "Well, do you think your statue saved us from a more serious bus crash?"

"Oh, I don't know. It did bring Guan Yin to mind, even though you don't believe that the statue is Guan Yin."

"Do you believe it is Guan Yin?"

"Sort of."

I heard a story once about a young woman in Japan who ran around with a statue of Guan Yin during the American bombing of Hiroshima. Someone told her that the statue wouldn't save her from the bombs, but she lugged it around anyway. She was found days later in a crumbled building. Dead, with the statue laying beside her in the rubble. That story always makes me shudder. I put Pocket Guan Yin back into my pocket. Hanne pulls out some peaches we brought from Lhasa.

"Mmm, peaches." I grab one and dust it off. I'm just about to take a bite when a man, a woman who's probably his wife, and a young girl approach. I have no idea where they appeared from, but they're looking at my peach.

"They might never have had a peach before, it's not like it's local fruit," says Hanne.

I give the little girl my peach and she smiles. The family's eyes move to Hanne's peach. She gives her peach to the little girl and we're left, peach-less, as the people disappear back to wherever they came from.

Tibetans in the countryside, like most "cultural minorities" in China, are poor. The Chinese government is apparently trying to raise their standard of living, but with a population of 1.3 billion and eighty percent of them living as peasants, the minorities have a way to go before the ideals of socialism become real in their lives.

It is said that the Tibetans and the Chinese may have both been nomads originally, but when the Chinese began to cultivate grains and became more static, the Tibetans continued as nomads, and the tribes split in 5000 BCE. Tibet's modern relations with China date back to the seventh century, when the two countries began correspondence and eventually began warring. The Tibetan empire grew and shrank and grew again over hundreds of years in every direction—east and south into China, north and west into the modern Xinjiang area. Buddhism was introduced and slowly became the religion of the ruling class here. The head of the Geluk School, the 5th Dalai Lama, held wide political control in the country in the seventeenth century, and other schools were forcibly converted to the Geluk mandate.

It seems as though, like most countries, Tibet had been fighting its neighbors for hundreds of years. In 1904, the British invaded via India. And the Chinese have been climbing onto this plateau forever it seems—generally under the pretense that Tibet is *part* of China. This all came to a head in 1950, when the People's Liberation Army entered Tibet and stayed. The Chinese government still maintains that it was a "Peaceful Liberation." I even went to an exhibition at the national museum in Shanghai entitled "Celebrating 50 Years of the Peaceful Liberation of Tibet." The exhibit displayed hundreds of Tibetan artifacts and ornate statues and jewelry from Tibet. I don't know how the goods were liberated, but "peaceful" is probably not the most appropriate adjective for describing the process.

After an hour of sitting beside the bus in the ditch, Hanne and I decided to walk to the larger road and hitchhike back to Lhasa. Eventually an SUV with the words "SAVE THE CHILDREN" painted on its side pulled up. The Tibetan man inside worked for the NGO and offered us a ride.

Lhasa sits in the basin of several mountains on the Plateau. Entering it feels like entering any small Chinese city: identical bike lane dividers line the streets, the same red and white patio stones cover the sidewalks, and most of the shops have Chinese writing. If you're not paying attention, you can forget you're in Tibet until you round a bend and it appears—soaring up above the city like it has grown from the earth by its own will—the Potala Palace. It sits on its rocky precipice across from a large communist square and several lines of Chinese shops blaring dance music. The Chinese city skirts and mocks the palace—bringing hundreds of Chinese migrants each year and floods of Western tourists.

The Potala Palace was built by the 5th Dalai Lama and was the seat of the Tibetan government until the 14th Dalai Lama's flight to India in 1959. Inside the palace is a maze of tall, dark rooms filled with enormous jeweled stupas holding the remains of the previous Dalai Lamas. There are rooms full of altars piled with statues with thousands of circumambulating Tibetans and hundreds of Western tourists pouring through every day. It is damp and dark and smells of yak butter and incense. Despite its sky-reaching position on the cliff, it has the same solid, earthy feel I've grown to appreciate in Tibetan architecture. But that doesn't mean it's without mystery. Inside the palace, I had the sense that no two rooms were on the same level. There were always steps to climb or descend when passing from one into the other. The roofs of each room were all varying heights, making the place more disorienting. I remember hearing that the 14th Dalai Lama used to play hide-and-seek in there as a child. It would be a fantastic building for hide-and-seek.

The place that I liked best in the palace was the Dalai Lama's private quarters. Though not private anymore, with the stream of tourists, the rooms were bright, windowed and had a warm, golden feel to them. Not to mention a fabulous view. After being in the Dalai Lama's room, I concluded that he must be a fine fellow because people who are not fine don't have rooms like that. All of that said, the bottom third of the Potala Palace is said to be dungeons—dungeons where people who have opposed the ruling party were kept in earlier centuries. I'm not sure how the current Dalai Lama feels about dungeons, but his earlier incarnations may not have been such clement chaps.

The Dalai Lama is apparently a manifestation of Chenrezig—Guan Yin. After each of his former selves dies, he reincarnates as another Dalai Lama. He has had some noble incarnations, but my favorite is the 6th

Dalai Lama, who was more of a minstrel than a monk and visited bars and brothels and wrote love poems. The 14th Dalai Lama now lives in Dharamsala, India, in exile. Many Tibetan people have followed him there and have built a colorful community in the area.

While the Dalai Lama remains the head of the Tibetan government, he seems to understand that the Chinese are never going to let go of Tibet. So he spends his time trying to improve life for the Tibetans, preaching liberty rather than independence. Of course, the Chinese government doesn't like him and has prohibited any photos or paintings of him to be shown in China—including, of course, Tibet. I have seen one exception: in the Tibetan Summer Palace, there is a mural of all the lives of the Dalai Lamas, painted with important events displayed. There is one for each incarnation, including the 14th. But the scene that is depicted is his meeting with Chairman Mao in 1954 in Beijing—as if that were the most important event in the 14th Dalai Lama's life.

I've often wondered why, if the Dalai Lama is an incarnation of Guan Yin, he would build dungeons in one incarnation, in another visit brothels, and in another still be exiled from his own homeland. Is it Guan Yin's way of saying, "Look, I'm here in all these places, too"? I'm not sure. I'll have to ask the Dalai Lama if I get a chance.

Hanne and I check into the guesthouse and set out to find some lunch in the Tibetan enclave. The enclave is built around the Jokhang temple—a major pilgrimage site for the Tibetans that was unfortunately used as a pigsty and barn during the Cultural Revolution. Walking past it any time of day, you can see numerous pilgrims prostrating in front of its doors or circumambulating its prayer-wheeled halls.

Outside the temple, the Barkhor Market is chock-full of stalls. Everything is for sale, from skull bowls lined with silver to imitation Ralph Lauren jackets. The market nauseates me and I feel guilty when I try to buy something and end up haggling in Mandarin with Tibetan vendors. In some ways I can't tell who is worse for Tibetan culture: Chinese emigrants who are here trying to earn a living or the Western tourists snapping pictures of the prostrating pilgrims. Maybe neither. Despite all of my humanitarian hopes for Tibet's liberation, now that I've seen the country, it's quite clear that the Chinese population and government are here to stay, and the West is hot on their heels, if the bus ride here was any indication. There was construction for hours and hours in the middle of nowhere—they're expanding the highway and finally finishing the railroad that Sun Yat Sen dreamed of at the turn of last century that will unify Tibet with the rest of China.

I follow Hanne to a potato stall. I've grown to love fried potato slices with a savory salt. And although the grease isn't good for my stomach, after the limited diet offered at the nunnery I think I'll risk it. Both Hanne and I are in good spirits now that we have our fried potato slices. We chew on them and weave our way through the market to visit Sanlin.

Sanlin is a Tibetan we met on the long bus ride from Xinning to Lhasa last week. We stopped at midnight 5000 meters up on one of the highest passes in the world. I floated out of the bus in the underwater middle of the night blue, nauseous with altitude and hunger. Hanne went inside to eat something and I stayed outside. I couldn't eat.

It took most of my energy to stay upright and I had the great urge to lean. So I leaned against the bus, observing the shapes of the mountains, the dark crags and lighter crags and military vehicles parked nearby in the icy moonlight.

Sanlin approached me. He wore a Boston Red Sox hat and Western clothes. He gave me a white silk scarf with Tibetan writing on it and said, "Welcome, friend." The scarf glowed in the moonlight as I put it around my neck, cool and soft. We stood and looked at each other and the shady mountains for a while in silence. I thought our conversation would end there as he didn't know English and I didn't know Tibetan, but it turned out that he spoke Mandarin and had been studying in Lanzhou for a few years.

I began to get queasy and decided that the best position to be in was horizontal, so I promised to speak with him once I felt a little better. I climbed on the bus and passed out until morning.

Sanlin visited us in our bunks and brought a white scarf for Hanne. That's when he told me that he was a statue maker. In fact, his entire family (well, the ones who haven't fled Tibet) make statues. I couldn't believe my luck: meeting a statue maker right in the middle of my statue crisis! Hanne wasn't as excited as I was—she was suspicious of Sanlin and thought he might be trying to rip us off. I imagined him and his family working in a dark factory, filled with molten metal, pouring little Taras, Buddhas and Guan Yins into moulds, everyone smiling, wearing baseball caps.

We have a map of how to find Sanlin's teacher's shop, but this is the first time that Hanne agreed to visit with me. The shop is behind a row of stalls selling fabric and raw meat. Beside the teacher's shop is another shop devoted solely to making clothes for statues: bright-colored embroideries to cover Buddhas and bodhisattvas during the cold winter months or for ceremonies. I peruse the clothes and wonder which would fit my Guan Yin statue back in Nanjing.

"This is strange. You're mad about statues and you manage to find people equally as mad as you. Imagine putting clothes on them like they're dolls," says Hanne.

Hanne isn't convinced about the importance of statues or images of god in general. I think her Lutheran upbringing is getting the better of her, especially in the face of some of the Bon images we've seen, with ghoulish deities wearing dismembered bodies for clothing. Or the old Bon temple we visited that had skulls and sinews painted around the doorways.

Here in Tibet I realize how much religious iconography is influenced by the culture and mindset of the people. Tibet has shown me the fiercer side of compassion. If I think of compassion as being whatever it takes to relieve someone from suffering, that might not always manifest itself in willow branches and purple bamboo groves—some illusions might take a sword or flames to cut through. Guan Yin in her multiheaded and multieyed manifestation as Chenrezig is appropriately represented here.

Sanlin is happy to see us and asks where we've been all week. Hanne and I peruse his co-workers' moulds and paints as they work on statues. They have a nice little setup and a garden where they can work outside. The sun streams in and I feel welcome.

"These are great!"

"Well, I'm not buying any," says Hanne, who for some reason or other is still suspicious of Sanlin. I think it's perfect timing that he appeared in the middle of my statue crisis.

"For goodness' sake, he's wearing a baseball cap on an angle like a gangster: what does he know about making gods and goddesses? This will be proof that your lady Guan Yin doesn't live in statues."

"I know she doesn't only *live* in statues. But I love the statues. I like his baseball cap. My lady Guan Yin lives in baseball too. She is everywhere."

"You are too clever for your own good. You know what I think? I think that the reason you like statues so much is because it's safe. It's very safe to love a statue," she says with a big smile.

Ouch. I almost brush off that comment, but it's one of those insidious ones that oozes into the cracks of my mind until I can think of nothing else. What exactly am I doing chasing an image around the globe?

We sit down on the little bench in the corner of the garden beneath a tree and finish our potato slices. Sanlin suggests that we take a trip outside of town to a lamasery where his teacher has been commissioned to build some statues. Hanne rolls her eyes.

Drepung Monastery was founded in 1416 and is about a ten-minute cab ride from downtown Lhasa. It's set partway up the mountain, with enormous boulders and green, green grass growing on all sides. Sanlin walks quickly; Hanne and I can barely keep up with him. We pass several groups of chubby middle-aged Westerners, panting from the altitude, some of them carrying cans of oxygen. Although it's July, it's cool in the shade of the lamasery's buildings, but when we enter the myriad courtyards the sun shines so bright and unimpeded it burns my eyes.

The tall, narrow corridors of the temple draw us in. We walk blind for several paces until our eyes adjust to the darkness. Sanlin leads us through meditation hall after meditation hall—soaring ceilings with colored banners dripping from such dark heights framing enormous statues of the Buddha and bodhisattvas and Padmasambhava. We eventually arrive at the hall where his teacher was commissioned to rebuild some statues.

For some reason, I had it in my head that the statues would be a couple of feet tall. I'm shocked to look up and see that the statues are about twelve feet tall, with gilded faces and ornate brush strokes on their contemplative eyebrows and eyes. The workers climb down off the ladders and greet Sanlin.

There are moulds for the statues' faces on the floor. Sanlin picks one up and hands it to me.

"*Pusa*," he says. It's the mould for the face of a bod-hisattva. So this is how they make them.

"That's quite something," says Hanne, clearly im-pressed by their work. "But it's also more proof that your Guan Yin doesn't live in statues."

Sanlin hands me the large plaster face of the bo-dhisattva in progress. I feel the plaster, imagine her with those compassionate eyes they'll paint on her. This will be another large room full of oversized images of bodhisattvas.

If I dropped the mould onto the floor it would become a pile of indistinguishable plaster. But that wouldn't mean that there isn't compassion in the world. I consider dropping it just to see what happens, but I'm immediately frightened by the idea. I give the face back to Sanlin and walk out of the hall.

Sanlin takes us to a room of *thangka*, many of which were painted by his teacher and his teacher's teacher. There are so many of them that there are not enough hooks to hang them, so they're layered on top of each other. *Thangka* are Tibetan paintings that help yoga or Buddhist practitioners with their meditations, similar to *yantra* or *mandala*, which are geometric, visual repre-sentations of a mantra or deity. These pictures give off the same rate of vibration as saying the deity's name or chanting a mantra. Making a *thangka* can take weeks of preparation and prayers to choose the appropriate deity and go through the necessary rituals. You're not supposed to rush a *thangka* painter. There are geometric considerations in laying out the paintings, as well as choosing the colors, and even the process of applying the paint can take weeks if done properly. In the end, the image is finally given eyes, and mantra is painted on the back to awaken it.

Although there are hundreds for sale in the market these days, Sanlin insists that there's a difference of intent between mass-produced *thangka* and these, created by a devout practitioner. Many of the *thangka* have veils to put over them when they're not being used—kind of like putting them to bed, so that the deities don't wander around the house uninvited. I peek under a few at the familiar faces of Tara and Padmasambhava. A Chinese guard tells me not to touch the paintings.

The next building we enter has a large painting of Chairman Mao on the wall. It's been whitewashed, but I can still read the writing underneath in the communist-style block letters and primary colors. I don't understand what it says, but the rendition of Mao has a certain revolutionary fervor to it. Someone likely painted it on the wall in the 1950s, when Mao ordered the army to unite Tibet with the rest of China or during the 1960s when the Cultural Revolution ravaged Tibet. It's almost the antithesis of the *thangka* I just saw. I have the urge to touch the painting but the hallway it's painted on is blocked off with bars.

Sanlin stands in the corridor between two tall white buildings and yells up to a tiny window three stories above. A little man pokes his head out and invites us upstairs.

We walk past the Chairman Mao painting again—this time on the inside of the bars. I drag my hand along it as we pass. I wonder how Chairman Mao felt as people turned his physical image into a symbol for the communist movement. Did he ever say, "No, stop, you're not seeing me for who I am—I'm just a man..."?

We climb to the roof. It's flat and burning bright, the sky azure. Two monks shave each other's heads among the golden spires overlooking Lhasa. The monks know Sanlin and welcome us. Sanlin says we're being given a special opportunity to meet a Living Buddha, although I don't know what the term means. The Living Buddha's assistant stands in the doorway. He's a wiry young guy and says that the Living Buddha is really old and may die soon but will give us a blessing because we are friends of Sanlin. He directs us to kneel beside the Living Buddha's bedside.

We enter the monk's chamber. I walk last. He has a humble room decorated in rich Tibetan colors, with a little bed and meditation box. Sanlin approaches the bed—baseball hat in hand. They speak in Tibetan.

While they chat, I get it into my head that I should give the monk my Pocket Guan Yin. I immediately disagree with myself and change my mind. What would an old Tibetan monk want with my Burmese Guan Yin? Besides, I reason that if this situation is a "play of empty being" then it doesn't really matter if I give the old monk the statue or not.

Hanne goes to meet him and my mind swings back and forth. I clutch and unclutch Pocket Guan Yin. I can't give the statue to the monk because I want to get rid of it or want to prove that I'm not attached to the form of Guan Yin—that's just like having an aversion to her.

It's my turn. I approach him and decide that I really do want to give him Pocket Guan Yin. It just feels right. So I do. I feel detached as I hand her to him. He looks at Pocket Guan Yin and mutters something and then looks at me.

I start speaking Chinese, then English, and then give up speaking. He looks at the statue for a long time. It seems like he's forgotten me. I decide to get up. But before I move, the old monk gives Guan Yin back to me with a big smile on his face.

I laugh and take the statue. I thank him in Chinese and then English and then leave. I can hear him laughing as I walk out onto the roof of the temple toward the stairs. The sky is the brightest bluest blue.

"You were in there for a while. What were you doing?" asks Hanne.

"I gave him my Pocket Guan Yin."

"Really? Good for you! That was a healthy thing to do, I think," she says proudly.

"He gave her back to me," I smile. She rolls her eyes.

We walk down the stairs from the Living Buddha's room, past the Chairman Mao painting, and enter the narrow, shaded corridors between the buildings once more. Sanlin says he's hungry and leads us toward the restaurant at the bottom of the monastery. Although they are finished serving for the day, they agree to feed us because we're with Sanlin. There's only one dish on the menu: rice, stewed indistinguishable vegetables and some grizzly meat mixed together.

We pick at our plates for a while but none of us eats very much. As I settle the bill, a Tibetan woman with a tattered maroon coat enters the restaurant asking for our scraps. Sanlin carefully scrapes all the leftover food from his plate, my plate and Hanne's plate into her gray plastic bag. The woman walks away smiling and I assume she is going to feed her dog.

When we exit the restaurant we meet the woman in the maroon coat again. She sits with her husband and four children on the ground below Drepung Monastery, eating our table scraps from the plastic bag. They take turns bringing the bag to their mouths, taking a bite and then passing the bag along to the next person.

Chapter 7

The Existential Crisis (Shanghai)
*Shanghai's antique market, the Jade Buddha Temple
and Lily-Awakened-to-Emptiness*

The small restaurant is empty except for the waitress and me and the buzzing of the overhead lights. I finished my *baizhou* and *youtiao* a while ago, and the jasmine tea is near cold in the paper-thin plastic cup. When I pick it up, the sides cave in, pushing the tea toward the brim threatening overflow. Flimsy transparency.

The waitress drops food remains from the other tables onto the floor with a gray rag and then mops the food into a pile with a gray mop, making tiny gray rivulets run variously across the tiles. Next she takes a plastic toilet-paper holder, one of which sits on most tables, pulls a long measure and dries the table beside me. She and I can't help but notice the same gray hue on the underside of the tissue.

My friend Matt flew to Australia this morning, leaving a gray world. When he got in the cab and drove away, it pulled my heart all the way up that tall Shanghai street. It's is all bent out of shape now.

That's the blessing and curse of this traveling. I meet people from around the globe, create a life in this strange context and when we part, our paths take us to opposite sides of the planet. Or in my case, leave me alone in one of the world's largest cities. Conversations turn to monologues—internal dialogues. The bubble created by a pair pops, and the world stares plainly at me.

Eight hours until my train leaves for Nanjing. I wander anonymously along the Bund, Shanghai's famous embankment along the Huangpu River. In the late 1900s this area was a major trading hub for Asia, with its curving sandstone buildings built by the French, the English, and the Americans when they thought they were going to make China their own. China belongs to no one.

To my left, across the river, sits Pudong—the Pearl Tower—and some of the tallest buildings in the world, shimmering on what was swamp twenty years ago. The scene, devoid of any mystical space, feels contrived and ridiculous today. The city's growth rate is staggering. There are cranes all over—hundreds of them building skyscrapers. God knows how many migrant workers from the countryside are living in squalor while working on fancy construction projects.

Shanghai. Shanghai is one of those cities where I have the sense that any material desire could be met with a little money and inclination. I don't have much of either right now, so I push forward, making a path along the Bund somewhere between China's bright future and the attempted colonial past.

A group of middle-aged women dressed in red sashes wielding bright red fans practice a dance overlooking the river. A small CD player by the railing accompanies them with a soaring *erhu* and *pipa*. The innocence and deliberation of their movements and the quivering notes slow my mind down. I don't know how long I watch their red fans twist and turn against the day.

I have that Sunday feeling: something fleeting, nagging on the edge of my mind, something that never was. A penumbra of nostalgia hangs over me. Nostalgia for what? I've been in China for over a year. I get tangled in various events and people for a time and always find myself alone in this wide place faced with my reason for being here—Guan Yin—searching for Guan Yin and finding only her absence. What is the lesson in searching for something and finding nothing?

I look over the railing into the murky brown river for the answer. Something approaches, soft and white, bobbing in the waves. I wait patiently as it comes closer:

a dead bloated goat. It bangs against the rocks and lurches downstream toward the East China Sea. I could disappear.

I walk. Off the Bund, the buildings are similar to those of old New York and Toronto—heavy stone, casting shadows, and creating breezes. I walk without destination, turning when I feel like it, avoiding the crowds on Nanjing Lu. Before long, I find myself in the Yu Yuan district, full of shops and tourists. What it is about people without destinations—we all seem to end up at the same places anyway.

This section of the city is a series of streets with traditional Chinese two-story buildings built in Ming and Qing style with whitewashed walls, red columns and soaring eaves. It used to be the red-light district and would swing at night with brothels, teahouses and gambling, old Chinese lanterns dangling everywhere. Nowadays it's an antique and trinket market where you can buy everything from silk and jade to faux Gucci.

Several low-rise wooden shops under lush trees sell revolutionary paraphernalia, including a porcelain statue of two Red Guards brandishing little red books and denouncing a school teacher as a counter-revolutionary. He kneels before them with a placard around his neck, announcing his wrongdoings, complete with a dunce hat. It's well preserved, not a chip on it, and the glaze shiny as the day it was fired. Why would anyone create a statue like this? I can't decide if it's a social commentary or if someone made it in support of the Red Guards. Maybe there's no difference. Isn't it funny that an image can live longer and have more meaning than the very thing it set out to represent?

Yesterday Matt and I came here to buy some souvenirs before his trip home to Melbourne. While we were shopping, I came across a stall selling candy-coated crabapples and other shiny fruit on sticks, all colorful and glazed in the evening light. Candy-coated crabapples are the best treat in China. They're one yuan each and seem to come out only at dusk. I had stopped to buy some when I heard Matt up ahead yelling, "Disco Guan Yin!"

Further down the lane there was an entire table covered in flashing singing disco Guan Yins, Guan Yin keychains, sparkly Guan Yin rings, Guan Yin hair-clips and massive Guan Yin pictures ringed with Christmas lights screaming colors and swirling mantra.

"What a bunch of junk," I said.

"I thought you liked Guan Yin," he said.

"I like refined Guan Yins. Art," I said. "Not kitsch."

"So you're telling me that a wooden Guan Yin is more Guan Yin than a disco Guan Yin?" asked Matt.

"I never thought of it that way. But I guess so," I spat out the seeds of my crabapple and took another bite.

"You're a snob," he smiled.

"You're right," I admitted. He was right.

We stood on the dim street chewing the crabapples and spitting the seeds at each other's feet. "I wonder how many times I've brushed elbows with Guan Yin in the past and missed her because of some idea in my mind? She has infinite forms, you know. She could be you, Matt."

"Or you," he replied.

The disco Guan Yin stall isn't here today. Matt isn't here either. In fact, Pocket Guan Yin isn't even here because before we left Nanjing I slipped her into Matt's backpack and sent her with him to Australia.

Today it isn't a matter of seeing Guan Yin's presence in myriad things—it's a matter of meeting absence. I pause for a moment on the narrow street between absent things. I imagine myself filled with absence, steeped in absence. And it dawns on me: absence is the wrong word. Absence implies that there is something missing. Nothing is missing; everything is exactly in its place, without reference.

Maybe being able to perceive Guan Yin in a multitude of forms isn't enough—I have to be able perceive her in formlessness. It is her compassionate way to reveal herself in whatever form is most expedient—for someone like me, who is fixated on a form, what could be more expedient than no-form? The thought is dizzying. I shudder.

Nothing feels particularly real any more. I walk. I try to forget everything that appeared before, I walk with a clear mind, not crowded by what I think should be, or what was yesterday or five minutes ago. This is the way I walk through a multitude of tiny lanes, with black-tiled roofs, moist courtyards, crawling plants and hanging clothes and then onto another street of one-story shops with rickety walls.

I recognize the street. I've been here before—last year. There aren't many tourists because it's out of the way. The store that I didn't want to see again stands before me. I could keep walking, but I have nowhere to go. I stand still. The open doors reveal about thirty large stone Buddha and bodhisattva heads on the concrete floor—decapitated heads for sale. Many with those tight Buddha curls, others with bodhisattva crowns. God knows where they came from. Some of their features are broken or worn away but for the most part they're intact.

The vendor man stands on the street in front of a table filled with smaller statues and trinkets. I stare past him at the heads—some face upward to the ceiling, others sideways stare at me, or maybe off into the void. Last year this sight upset me—these are refined bodhisattva heads, antiques, likely lifted from some temple or religious grotto. Last year I wanted to rescue them, take them away and preserve them.

The vendor man steps up onto the heads and moves toward the back of the shop. He walks carefully, so as not to injure the faces. He takes a small teapot off the back shelf, pours himself a steaming cup and sips it, standing upon two heads. A year ago this shop upset me. Today it mocks me. I stand still.

My feet don't feel like they're touching the ground anymore. The heads invite me closer, giggling, "What are you looking at? We don't mean anything—have a cup of tea!" Their beatific smiles grow wide like ringing bells and then turn sinister. They laugh. The laughter gets louder and louder as everything joins in—the little jade carvings, the Chinese books I can't read, the statues of Chairman Mao, the statues of Guan Yin. All laughing—a cacophony of laughter and decapitated bodhisattva heads.

"*Fo tou* (Buddha heads)," the voice says, puncturing my balloon. My heart thumps high in my chest and head. I'm suddenly aware that it was me who was laughing.

"*Pusa tou* (bodhisattva heads)," I respond to the voice.

"Oh, you can speak Chinese."

"Yeah," I turn and face the voice. She smiles. She's wearing a jean jacket and jeans, a wide-collared pink shirt, sunglasses on top of her head and cool white sneakers. She looks too fashionable to be a vendor here.

"What are you laughing at?" she asks.

"My life."

"It is very funny?"

"Yeah."

"You are lucky, many people do not have very funny lives."

Yes. We leave the Buddha heads and continue up the street like we've known each other for years. Her name is Lily; she was born in the year of the Pig. I'm a Rabbit, so decidedly we'll get along easily.

We stop at a bubble tea stall and buy hot bubble tea with extra tapioca balls in it. Its milky sweetness warms me but my favorite part is squishing the little balls in my mouth. Lily's straw is bright pink, mine deep blue. She drinks quickly, the balls whipping up her straw, making her seem younger than she is as she speaks with them stuck in her teeth.

She's Taiwanese and here on a business trip. Her family is originally from Shanghai but immigrated to Taiwan in the 1940s. She has the day off before flying back to Taiwan and plans to visit the Jade Buddha temple because she once visited it with her mother when her mother was alive. She wants me to come with her. I begin to shake my head—I don't want to visit any temples today. I've seen enough of images of the Buddha and bodhisattvas, and I don't understand form.

"I've seen enough Buddhas today. I don't want to see any more. I don't understand form," I say.

"The Jade Buddha is not form, he is non-form," she says. She slurps the last pile of tapioca balls up her straw, squishes them in her teeth.

"If he's non-form then why go see him?" I ask.

"Because he is beautiful," she says. "We'll take a taxi."

We take a cab across town to look at formless beauty. The cab driver is an amiable man, though not the smoothest driver. He keeps looking in the rearview mirror at me instead of the road. When I lived in Canada I always wore a seatbelt. I've given up even looking for one in Chinese cabs. Particularly in the back seat; they're always covered with white sheets, making the atmosphere feel clean.

There's a fashion show on the sidewalk: three tiny women with large breasts dance in tall leather boots and dry ice. The music—bad techno—spills into our cab and lingers as we drive away. Shanghai rambles on, broad avenue after broad avenue, towering skyscrapers, unique modern architecture, Western enclaves behind gates—cosmopolitan and beautiful. It radiates the same way New York and London do.

The Treaty of Nanjing of 1842 opened Shanghai for international business and the opium and the gambling and the prostitution rings that came with it. The British, French, American and other expats were allowed to live here and not be subject to Chinese law. They ran their own concessions until the 1940s. But after the communists overthrew the Gumingdong in 1949, Shanghai's thriving business sections dissolved or lay dormant under the communist rule. It wasn't until Deng Xiao Peng's Open Door Policy was instated in the 1980s that the city began to flourish once more. These days nothing holds it back. Many Chinese people that I've spoken to say it is the new Hong Kong, but better than Hong Kong. There's a steady stream of international companies entering the city and thousands of expatriates who have made Shanghai home. The city is under construction twenty-four hours a day.

Lily and I jostle around in the back seat discussing the *Journey to the West*—the book I'm currently reading and one of China's most famous novels. The book is a fictional account of Xuanzang's journey to India. Xuanzang lived in the seventh century and was the founder of the "Mind Only" School of Buddhism. He translated hundreds of texts and is revered as a great teacher in China.

In Journey to the West, the fictional character of Xuanzang travels with three companions through vast landscapes for many years to bring back the Buddhist scriptures. They undergo hundreds of trials on the way and encounter demons that try to kill them and gods or Buddhas who try to help them. The book is full of poems and metaphors for the spiritual path.

Guan Yin is in the book and is, of course, my favorite character.

Lily's favorite character, of course, is Sun Wu-kong—the Monkey King. She says that most people don't understand the esoteric meaning of his name or the story because they read only abridged versions and think he's all acrobatics and charm. But Monkey King's name is *Wukong*, which means "awakened to emptiness." Lily seems to be obsessed with emptiness, if that's possible. She keeps saying "awakened... to emptiness" over and over again. I begin to wonder if she isn't as crazy as I.

The Jade Buddha Temple is on An Yuan Road in the northwestern part of the city. We pass through its ochre gate to the main complex, built in the style of the Song Dynasty, with symmetrical courtyards and moon doors, sky-turned eaves and bright yellow walls. I want to stay in the courtyard; there's something about the layout that calms me. I don't want to see any statues, of that I'm sure.

I focus on the group of pilgrims in their matching yellow bags and white tennis shoes lighting incense through the moon door. Moon doors are my favorite architectural element in China. They are literally doors shaped like moons, complete circles cut out of walls that you get to pass through when entering a courtyard or temple. The first moon door I saw was in Mochu Park, in the garden leading to the house where the pretty girl whom the park was named after lived. Apparently she drowned herself for some reason in the lake near her house and so it was called Don't Be Sad Lake. Although there are moon doors all over China, I can't help but associate them with the sweetness and sadness of the young girl who drowned in Don't Be Sad Lake.

Lily stands beside me reading steles. I try to ignore her, but she points out the Guan Yin one with the *Heart Sutra* carved above her. The sutra where Guan Yin realizes that *matter is not different from void and void is not different from matter—void is matter, matter is void*. Emptiness! A sutra that I can rhyme off in two languages but don't understand—the words mean nothing. I turn away and cover my head with my hands and look at the ground between my shoes.

"Why don't you want to see the Buddha?" Lily asks.

"I'm tired of statues and ideas—they mock me and don't mean anything. Remember those decapitated Buddha heads in the market—I looked at them and they all meant nothing—they were empty. I have no frame of reference today. I'm sick of religious images and nothing makes any sense," I whine.

"Of course the Buddha heads are empty—they are Buddha heads. Buddha is empty like Sun Wukong and Guan Yin," she laughs. I frown. "You see, empty head is good, but it's not the head that's so important. Everyone always wants to empty the head. But they think too much and focus too much on the head. It's the heart that needs to be open, empty—*kong*. You can't have a full heart—it has to be empty so that there is room for the breeze to blow and *all* things to fit inside. The *pusa* have empty hearts; that is how they love the whole world," she says confidently.

I've never thought of it that way before—empty hearted *pusa*? My heart is stretched out of shape today, maybe a little empty in spots. I wonder how much my heart could hold if it were completely empty.

Lily walks to another stele and I wonder where she came from. She's a bit of a philosopher, I think. An undercover philosopher, the way she pontificates in her denim outfit and sunglasses. Appearance tells me nothing. Maybe she's a bodhisattva.

This is one of the charms of traveling alone—meeting people. When I'm alone, there's openness in me that allows for something new to enter—or should I say emptiness.

"Are you a *Pusa*, Lily?"

"Come and visit Jade Buddha. You can close your eyes, you don't have to look," she says.

"Okay, but you'll have to guide me," I say, entrusting myself to her once more.

We enter the queue at the right-hand side of the hall and I close my eyes and giggle. When it's our turn, Lily leads me in front of the Jade Buddha. It's quiet except for some faint murmurs in the hallway. Lily breathes audibly, clearly moved by his presence. I feel a light breeze and a buzzing in my chest—I have to peek. My hair stands on end when I see his luminous form. He's the prettiest and saddest thing I've ever seen. I want to touch him in his milky splendor. He's about five feet tall, sitting in the lotus position of non-fixation. My eyes water as Lily and I float out of the hall into the sunny courtyard. Everything feels more alive than earlier, even inanimate things seem to pulse as if they have love of their own coursing through them.

"Beautiful and empty both," she says. I nod and think about the monk who transported the statue all the way from Burma in 1882—across the continent with one ton of Buddha.

"The lengths we go for a form representing emptiness..." I muse.

"Not so far as you came for a form representing compassion. You could have stayed home and Guan Yin would be there, you know. She is a wave."

Lily isn't the first person to say this to me. Several wise people have also said it—I've even thought it myself. But thinking gets me nowhere.

"Tell me more about this Guan Yin wave and how I should have stayed at home," I say.

"Yes. But I am hungry," announces Lily. "How about sushi? We'll take a taxi." I follow her out of the saffron temple onto the Shanghai streets.

In the taxi, Lily tells me about her brother, a practicing Daoist monk in Taiwan, and then gives me a small crystal that he excavated from a cave near his monastery. She says that he would like me because I like Guan Yin. Even though he is a Daoist, he loves Guan Yin. She then insists that Taiwan has preserved the Chinese religions that were destroyed during the past fifty years on the mainland. "Daoism and Buddhism are alive in Taiwan—we have a strong culture and respect for religion," she says, "but the Chinese government thinks we are merely a province of China. We are not!" Most Taiwanese people I've met in China have a great contempt for the Chinese government and think it's ridiculous that it will not recognize them as an independent nation.

Like Tibet, Taiwan (the Republic of China) is seen as a province of China. But unlike Tibet, Taiwan has its own army, nuclear weapons, and economy and has been independent of China since the Gumingdong migrated there in 1949 with most of the of the mainland's gold and cash.

The sushi restaurant is crowded, but we find a pleasant low table in the corner beneath a blue lantern. Lily orders some tea and asks me for my notebook. She writes

Guan Shi Yin, and then crosses out the *shi* and writes the suffix *qi* instead. I don't know what she's getting at.

"Guan Yin is a wave," she says. "She is supersonic, and the essence of all sounds—all things. She is inside the sounds, and she is the sound inside—the wave of love, the echo of silence in the open heart. Maybe like the Jade Buddha is the emptiness inside the beauty."

"Or the beauty inside the emptiness."

"Exactly."

Our tea arrives and the waitress pours us each a cup. My cup is thin, rimmed with a pale green glaze like the Jade Buddha. Lily's is an electric red. The tea, aromatic and hot, tickles right through me. I am suddenly overcome with gratitude for my meeting with Lily. What are the chances of running into someone on a Shanghai street that loves Guan Yin as much as I do?

"Isn't it neat that we both like Guan Yin and we met on that street?" I muse.

"Who would you expect to meet—someone who isn't friends with Guan Yin? I told you she is a vibration. When you tune into her wave she takes you everywhere, you meet her everywhere—because she *is* everything—in form, in not form," she says pointedly. "I have to go to the toilet." She stops at the counter and discusses something with the waitress and then disappears down the hallway.

I sip my tea and think about the Guan Yin frequency. I imagine myself tuning in like a radio, picking up some fuzz and static until slipping into her wave. Emptiness—openness seems to be her main channel, lots of room for her to vibrate in. I tune my heart to that frequency and close my eyes.

The waitress brings me a steaming white towel to wash my face and hands. I melt into its heat and then another waitress arrives with a wooden boat full of sushi. There's enough food here to feed several people, multicolored tiers with shimmering vegetables and bright decorative flowers. She pours me a fresh cup of tea, and a little dish of soy sauce, then picks up Lily's cup and walks away.

"Ni gan shen me?" I call out, referring to Lily's cup. The waitress turns around confused.

"Ni de pengyou zou lu," she says.

"Shen me?"

Lily paid the bill and left several minutes ago.

I could run outside and look for her but I know I'd never find her. A warm wave washes through me as I look down the hallway where her vaporous presence disappeared. I haven't felt this calm in a long time.

I sit alone in the soft light with my jade-green cup and the enormous spread of sushi. The dark wooden chopsticks are smooth in my hand as I stir some wasabi into the soy sauce and then place a thin slice of pickled ginger on an avocado roll. I lift the piece deliberately, give it a good soak in the wasabi and soy sauce mix and then pop it into my mouth.

Chapter 8

⚜

Lao She Teahouse (Beijing)

Tiananmen Square and discussions with some philosophers
at Lao She Teahouse

Nanjing is, unfortunately, positioned on the southern shore of the great Yangzi River, which makes it part of southern China, and southern China isn't heated. So during the winter months, everyone wears winter coats indoor and dreams of spring. In my classroom at the university where I teach part-time, all the students wear winter coats; you can see your breath because the windows are often left open for "circulation." I conduct my classes in a wool hat and wear a woolen sweater under my winter coat. But no matter how many layers I put on, the damp cold still gets to me.

My apartment is no better. I attempted for weeks to warm it with small space heaters and wasn't successful. The only place I was warm was in bed, so I spent most of my days there last month when I wasn't working. I was quite willing to pass the entire winter that way until a few days ago, when an abominable force entered the apartment. My roommate, Simon, foolishly allowed his girlfriend, Ling, to stay in his room while he went home to England for a month and Ling, in turn, invited her mother to come from Wuhan to stay with us for two weeks over Christmas and Western New Year.

Ling's mother had been in the apartment for only an hour before she took over the place. The first thing she did was unplug all the heaters. She then proceeded to open the door to the balcony and all of the windows so that a gale blew through the place. I began to think that she was mad, sitting there in the darkness because she didn't want to waste electricity. Ling explained that her mother had been sent to a labor camp as a teenager during the Cultural Revolution and never quite recovered: although the family has a decent income, she's extremely frugal and never turns on the heat and tries to avoid using lights at night.

At the mention of "labor camp" I grew sympathetic and retired to my room, where I climbed into bed and used the lights and space heater and tried to forget about Ling's mother. About an hour later, I went into the kitchen to get a drink and found the fridge door standing open and all the food missing. I looked around the kitchen for signs of my grapefruit juice, but there was nothing on the counter. My curiosity drew me into

Simon's room, where I found the entire contents of the fridge sprawled across his large wooden desk: half a chicken in its greasy fat, tofu from the night before, half a dozen oozing Styrofoam containers, my grapefruit juice and various condiments. Ling and her mother were huddled together under several blankets on Simon's bed watching a Chinese soap opera—apparently TV wasn't a waste of electricity!

I stared at Ling and then back at the desk, awaiting an explanation. "Mama says that it's cooler in the apartment than the fridge, so there's no point in wasting the electricity to cool the food. So we unplugged the fridge and took the food out." They both stared at me blankly, as if I were the one who didn't understand.

I knew then that nothing could save me from the cold except a trip to China's north—where rumor had it they used heaters. I walked back into my room, packed a bag, went to the train station, bought an overnight ticket to Beijing, and left Ling and her mother to their southern winter antics.

Beijing has an interesting shape. It's circular, radiating from the Forbidden City in rings toward the suburbs. Architecture swings from tiny white-walled *siheyuan* (four houses around a walled garden) to towering skyscrapers to new housing with fifty-year life expectancy to elaborate temples and imperial palaces and tombs of emperors. It has an international feel with all of the embassies and foreigners. But most importantly for me, in my attempt to escape the cold of the south, many places in Beijing are heated. And even outdoors, I find myself in proper dry cold.

I'm not a particularly industrious tourist, but I've made my way this afternoon to the center of Beijing. Here is the Forbidden City, its immense terra-cotta walls, sprawling courtyards and gleaming yellow roofs laid out with precision, each archway and gate facing south, signifying the symmetry of all things in relation to the various emperors who lived here. Nowadays, no emperor reigns inside, but Chairman Mao's photo smiles above the main gate, watching over Tiananmen and the whirling boulevard that surrounds it.

Across the road from the Forbidden City is Tiananmen Square, its icy, wide grounds glossy in the sun like fresh white paint. A handful of kites flash above the square in the sun, marring an otherwise flawless milky-blue sky. I watch them until my neck hurts. One of the most noble pastimes in China is kite flying—all major cities and just about every park within them seem to host at least one flyer. Even at night you can see kites soaring high above the city, with little red blinkers marking their place among the skies. I'm relieved to find that Tiananmen is no exception. Even though covered in ice and snow and haunted by ghosts of protests past, Tiananmen has a healthy supply of kite aficionados, rivaled in number only by patrolling guards who ensure that no one stalls too long in one spot and no one carries anything flammable with which to douse themselves in protest. Assessing the situation of the square, I reckon that if I were a political dissident, I would disguise myself as a kite flyer—they seem to be allowed to go about their business of flying without much interference by the guards. In fact, I begin to see their flying as a political act, though clearly the guards haven't picked up on the new revolution.

Tiananmen is apparently large enough to hold a million people, though I doubt whether more than twenty could gather in a group without being dispersed by the furry-collared guards. In the southern end of the square stands the reason for today's visit: Chairman Mao's Mausoleum. The pillared granite building was constructed with materials from all over China—including sand from the Taiwan Strait and rocks from Mount Everest—and represents China's far-reaching grasp.

By the time I remove myself from kite watching, there's already a long queue outside of the mausoleum (the only place in the square you can stand in a group and not be questioned). The majority of the people in line are Chinese, but there are a few Westerners too, including the couple directly in front of me.

"I'm not waiting in line to see a mass-murderer!" he says.

"Then wait out here, because I am," she says. They both wear dark blue duffle coats, not unlike mine.

"You're going to pay your respects to a murderer?" he asks.

"Who said anything about paying respects?" she says. "But, you know, I've read a lot of Chinese history and I don't remember reading that Mao was ever convicted of murder."

"Yeah, he and Hitler never laid a hand on anyone."

"You can wait out here then, Jeremy. I want to see the building, and I want to see the Chairman," she says.

"Sick," he says and walks away, though not very far. He pulls out a package of cigarettes and lights one. She looks to me for some kind of support. I guess I'm also "sick" for waiting to see Mao.

"He thinks I'm a Maoist," she says to me.

"Are you?"

"Of course not. But I don't think that Chinese people are stupid. There must have been some things that Mao did right or there's no way this would have been built," she points toward the building.

It amazes me to see the lengths the party has gone to keep Mao as a central symbol: he's on all of the money now, and there's paraphernalia everywhere with his face on it. And they've got him lying in state in this building, where people come and pay respects.

Mao Zedong became well known after leading the communist party to victory over the Gumindong in 1949. He was an idealist and a poet and spoke of equality, Marxist ideals, and the development of China as a great unified nation. But during his reign as political head of China, some of his policies went severely awry, and millions of people perished from famine and persecution. He is a highly controversial character, and although the Chinese government has clearly moved on since his reign and death in 1976, his image still haunts the country.

"Do you think that maintaining the image of Mao as a revolutionary hero is a way for the government to maintain control?" I ask.

"Yes, I think that's true. And I think it's fascinating what people choose to believe. So yes, I want to go in that building and see what they've done with him, the same way I'd go into a church in Europe to see what they've done to Jesus or the other saints."

"Oh, you're not comparing Mao to Jesus again, are you Alice?" asks Jeremy.

"What if I am? They're both symbols of salvation, aren't they? Don't they both stand for salvation? Mao lead millions of people out of feudal slavery. What has Jesus done for anyone lately?" she laughs. "But anyway, my point is that both Mao and Jesus have been symbols for emancipation."

Jeremy walks away again, and I'm left wondering about the relationship between Mao and Jesus.

Two security guards make their way down the line, instructing us that we can't bring bags into the mausoleum. Jeremy grudgingly agrees to hold them for us.

"Watch this." Alice says. She buys some colorful silk flowers from the lady beside the queue. "For the Chairman," she smirks.

"You are such an ass," Jeremy says.

"My brother thinks he's a pacifist, but really he's just an angry man, like most people pretending to be pacifists," she whispers. We enter the gate and leave Jeremy behind.

The mausoleum is bright—lots of windows and an enormous white marble statue of the Chairman in front of an elaborate woolen tapestry describing the beauty of the homeland. It has that stifling sterility that all mausoleums possess. I want to hold my breath so as not to breathe it in.

There's a metal table where mourners place their multicolored silk flowers. Alice drops hers among the others, and I realize that they will be resold to the next group of mourners—not a bad setup. A feeling of irony permeates the place.

We're asked not to speak, so we pass silently into Mao's chamber, where he lays prone in his blue-gray suit in a crystal casket. I get about a two-second glance at him because we are paraded through so quickly, but I have the distinct feeling that he has a low-wattage light-bulb in his head because he glows slightly. Or maybe the lightbulb is symbolic of all of his bright ideas. I've heard rumors that when Mao died, the body was pumped with too much formaldehyde and his face swelled beyond recognition; they eventually got him back into shape, but made a wax version just in case something else went wrong. No one knows if the Mao on display is waxen or not. Either way, he looks like most corpses I've seen: leathery and puffy—an imitation of a man.

We exit the south side of the building into glaring sun on snow. Jeremy waits for us, seemingly in a better mood. "What did he look like? Was it a real corpse?"

"Why don't you go in yourself if you're so curious?" Alice responds. But after a plaintive look from Jeremy, she tells him everything in great detail. I can see that although they tease each other, the duffle-coat-wearing couple get along very well. I take my bag from Jeremy, walk toward the kite flyers, and think about shapes: the shapes we pray to and the shapes we create to represent an idea or an ideal. Chairman Mao is nothing but a symbol now, but a symbol for what? His airbrushed portrait hanging above the entrance to the Forbidden City doesn't answer.

What Alice says rings true in some way: without the help of Lin Biao and his great efforts to turn Mao into a cult figure during the 1960s, the Chairman may have never risen to such epic proportions. It was Lin who compiled Mao's revolutionary aphorisms into books and made it a policy for every member of the People's Liberation Army to study Mao's sayings.

A long and steady indoctrination of people who were eager to believe in something gained Mao more strength as a political and ideological leader, and Lin was wise in his methods. He got people on the ground interested in the Chairman: the soldiers, the commoners. By the time the Cultural Revolution flourished, Mao was already held as a kind of god in Chinese minds: untouchable, floating above the everyday drudgery, promising a bright future, almost like a heavenly father who watched over the lives of the communists.

Mao was the kind of god that you couldn't refute without paying a heavy price: countless intellectuals and counterrevolutionaries were forced to study his sayings and confess to crimes against the Chinese Communist Party's (CCP)'s policies in labor or thought-reformation camps. Those who couldn't convince the interrogators of their sincere devotion to Mao and the party were severely punished, even killed. It wasn't Mao himself carrying out these atrocities—he was a symbol for a much larger movement and struggle for power.

It does sound a little like the Crusades. Maybe Mao could be compared to Jesus, as Alice suggests: arguably his followers, namely the Christians and their various churches, perverted Jesus's message, too. By now the couple have caught up with me, and I mention this to Alice. She lights up and says, "Bravo, my thinking exactly!" She and Jeremy invite me to walk the *hutong* with them for the afternoon, and we leave the bright square for the narrow lanes.

We spend a couple of hours wandering through Beijing's traditional laneways and houses—the *hutong* and *siheyuan*. Many of the narrow, white-walled and black-roofed streets that once covered the city are being torn down to build high-rises to suit the growing population, modernization schemes, and approaching Olympics. But some, especially around the city core, remain as a testament to China's past, with granite streets and wooden doorways into small, shared gardens and damp, short houses. Even in winter, people mill about on the narrow streets, and bikes stand in the icy lanes. Like everything in modern China, there are mixed feelings about the tearing down of the *hutong*. Many people don't want to leave their old homes and move into tall apartment buildings where everyone becomes a stranger. And Westerners particularly don't want to see the charms of

China's past destroyed. But at the same time, many of the old houses are dilapidated, with no insulation or cement floors, so there are some basic benefits in the anonymous, suburban apartment blocks.

Throughout the *hutong* there are many food vendors selling everything from candy-coated fruit, to taffy Chinese zodiac symbols on sticks. But most interesting to me are the two young female tea sellers from southern China. They are teenagers and both have such rosy, innocent faces as they approach with long sticks on their shoulders, balancing large baskets of tea. We all buy tea from them because they are so sweet and look so cold.

The younger of the two weighs the tea and bags it in small paper bags, smiling shyly, while the older does all the talking. She tells me that they are staying with an uncle who owns a tea shop and this is how they are earning a living. I ask if they plan to go to university, and they just laugh and smile—no. The poor in China are still poor, despite all the revolutionary hopes for equality in the past hundred years. And the people of the countryside don't often attend school after middle school—and university is out of the question. Like so many waitresses and construction workers I've met in Nanjing, these girls have moved to the city to find jobs to send money back home to their families. In a couple of years they will return to their village and get married.

The sun is low and casts a weak pink light over the stony streets as we make our way back to Qianmen. We decide to go for some tea to warm up at Lao She Teahouse. The teahouse is named after the playwright and novelist Lao She, but there is a pun involved because he actually had a play called *Teahouse*. Lao She was a political writer and a socialist, but like many intellectuals of his time, he was eventually persecuted and, some say, murdered. Others say he was driven to suicide by the Red Guard. Either way, he died during the Cultural Revolution. His famous novel is *Camel Xiangzi*—a tragedy about the doomed life of a rickshaw driver in Beijing. Xiangzi represented China's working poor and no matter how hard he tried, he couldn't raise his standard of living. It makes me think of the two tea sellers in the *hutong*: I hope that they somehow break the cycle of poverty. But as we enter the large, warm tearoom filled with Westerners and wealthy Chinese, the ghost of *Camel Xiangzi* mocks my hopes.

I'm not sure why this teahouse is named after Lao She, because it's clear that this place specializes in Beijing Opera. The staircase leading up to the second floor is filled with pictures and paraphernalia of Beijing Opera, and as much as I enjoy twanging instruments and soaring squealing voices, I'm not in the mood for them tonight. I ask the hostess about the opera and she says it starts later. Good.

We sit facing the stage at a chunky wooden table. On the stage, two women musicians—a *guqin* and an *erhu*, play a slow, sad song. They're both dressed in long red *qipas*. The *erhu* player seems to be having a good time as she whines out her song, but the *guqin* player frowns as she bends her long notes. Red lanterns dangle and trapped cicadas chirp in tiny bamboo cages above the tables. Jeremy and Alice both light up cigarettes, adding to the mood of the place.

The waitress arrives with a selection of strange nibbles and a pot of tea that Jeremy chose. She pours us each a glass then dumps the contents of the glass back into the teapot to warm up our cups and move the tea around. Then she pours us each another cup and walks away.

We drink our tea. It's smooth, almost nutty, and comes from Anhui province. Outside the window, the sky has turned pale salmon fading into white and then icy blues. There isn't a cloud in the sky. I begin to feel particularly Chinese sitting here and have a great urge to light up a cigarette. Jeremy, Alice and I smoke in silence, listening to the cicadas and the small band.

"That man is rude," says Jeremy, referring to the man at the table beside us. The man is in the process of telling the waitress off for not pouring his tea properly.

Apparently you're supposed to pour half of the cup full and then let it sit for a time before filling it completely. The waitress is embarrassed and has turned bright red. The gentleman stands up and uses his girlfriend's cup to show the waitress the proper way to pour tea. The waitress scuttles away and I can see her by the counter, likely recounting the tale to her friends.

The man's girlfriend begins to tell him off to the nods of Alice and Jeremy. Their argument grows so loud that it threatens to upstage the *erhu* and *guqin* concert. The woman stands up, grabs her lime-green purse and storms out of the teahouse, leaving the man alone at his chunky table. He notices us noticing him and smiles.

"She cannot take me anywhere," he says in perfect English.

He has a twinkle in his eye but doesn't seem as confident as he did a couple of minutes ago. We smile and turn back to our tea. Jeremy doesn't like the gentleman but Alice seems to find him rather charming, and before I know it she's invited him to sit with us. Alice and Jeremy seem quite adept at picking up strangers, and here I thought I was special. We move our clumsy chairs aside and make room for him at the table. "It was she that wanted to come here, not me, and now she's left. And I don't care for teahouses," he says.

"But you care for tea," says Alice.

"Yes, I care for tea, but not shows," he says. We all look at the small stage to witness the show he doesn't care for. The concert continues in its wiggling notes and soaring strings. The *guqin* player's eyes keep drifting towards the clock on the wall as if she's looking there for inspiration.

The man's name is Yuhong—meaning "Red Universe." He does some kind of multimedia work in Beijing. I've heard a variety of cultural revolutionary names such as "little soldier" and "general" and "red this and that," but '"red universe"? Clearly his parents were caught up in revolutionary fervor when he was born. I wonder if they were Red Guards.

"Were your parents supporters of the revolution?" I ask.

"Yes, and I'm a supporter of the revolution still," he responds.

"What revolution would that be?" asks Jeremy.

"Any revolution that will keep China pure and free from outside control. Besides, we have a long history of revolutions here in China—if something isn't working, we overthrow it. But we are patient, like a river, ever flowing, and no foreign power will ever take over our China," he says. He lights himself a cigarette.

"You can't possibly think that the Cultural Revolution was a positive revolution," says Jeremy. He's getting the same hurt look in his eyes that he had when I met him and Alice and she was on her way into Mao's Mausoleum.

"In the revolution, what was done needed to be done in order to save China," Red Universe says.

"What about the Hundred Flowers Campaign?" I ask. Red Universe is quiet and seems lost in thought.

Chairman Mao initiated the Hundred Flowers Campaign. In attempts to unify various factions of the Chinese population, he asked the intellectuals, poets and scientists to come forward and air their grievances toward the CCP. It took a while before anyone was brave enough to do it, but eventually thousands of well-educated people began publishing articles, writing plays and holding discussions about what was wrong with the party and how they had been mistreated.

This continued for some time, until local administrators of the CCP got angry. They in turn contacted the higher administration in Beijing and pressure mounted on Mao. Mao then refuted his initial argument that people should be able to air grievances and restated that they should be publishing only works that supported the party. Chaos and persecution ensued—hundreds of thousands of educated Chinese people were deemed counterrevolutionaries and exiled to labor and reformation camps.

"During the 1950s, 1960s, and 1970s, there were too many smart and influential people in China. Some of them had to leave and had to be dealt with or they would have disturbed the whole," says Red Universe finally.

"You think intellectuals were a threat to your country?"

"Yes. Chairman Mao did everything he could to save our country from outside control or from foolish people on the inside who couldn't see the bright future ahead for China. He knew that if your arm is sick—if your arm has cancer—you cut it off to save the rest of your body."

Something about that metaphor sounds too pragmatic to me. I begin to feel squeamish talking to Red Universe. "You compare the intellectuals and artists in China during the revolution to a sick arm?" I ask.

"Yes," he says. He sips his tea.

"It was the brain of China that was cut out!" fumes Jeremy.

"And why are you visiting our China?" Red Universe changes the topic. It feels like he's gathering information rather than just being friendly. Jeremy and Alice explain their train trip through Russia and Mongolia and finally China. And I try to explain that I'm looking for, or rather researching, Guan Yin bodhisattva. And then we all fall silent and listen to the cicadas in their cages and watch the frowning *guqin* player.

Red Universe starts up again. "During the Cultural Revolution, people all over China were looking for hope. They had very little hope, they had been starving—there had been great drought. They wanted something to believe in, a plan that would get them through, and they thought that destroying or persecuting counterrevolutionaries and images of the past was part of a greater cause."

"What cause was that?" I ask.

"You think that Guan Yin is a cause to believe in, something outside of yourself that you act in accordance with and it brings about an outcome, correct?"

I nod.

"Well, the Cultural Revolution destroyed only a million people and preserved China from the rest of the world for thirty years. Now we are entering the world market on our own terms. Many sacrifices were made for a much larger cause. This becomes more clear with each passing year."

I try to think in generations instead of individual lives and realize that my brain probably isn't wired for it. I've heard stories from the Cultural Revolution of people going to prison and thought reformation for ridiculous reasons, like my friend Yun's grandfather. He ran the film projector at a local cinema and fell asleep one night while showing a film about Chairman Mao. There was an electrical fire and both the projector and the film burned up. He went to prison for five years for defacing a Chairman Mao film.

"I can't believe that you talk about human beings like they're some kind of system, some kind of statistic that needs to be manipulated and controlled," says Jeremy.

"Only fools speak out against the government, only selfish people. Our party was and is doing what's best for China's future, and if people cannot see this they should keep quiet," says Red Universe.

Outside the window, it's black now. But I know that Tiananmen, the Gate of Heavenly Peace, home of protests past, looms across the street and mocks anyone who would dare protest in it today. What Red Universe says is probably true—only fools would speak out against the government—but that doesn't mean that the people of China don't think. Surely the purging of intellectuals and artists during the Cultural Revolution kept the masses under control for a couple of decades, but could educational and fear-based control be so thorough that there are no dissenters left? I look at Red Universe: he's a well-educated, fully bilingual intellectual. He tows the party line, but does he actually believe it? How long before there's another revolution in China? I remember a Chairman Mao poem that says, "Man's world is mutable, seas become mulberry fields." The Chinese have a way of looking at things that we in the West often fail to see.

"In China we don't deal with individuals—we deal with the group, we see what is best for the whole. We don't look at one life, or one lifetime, we look at generations. Why do Westerners always want to separate themselves? What makes you think that you are special? Intelligent people know that the world is not so interested in one man. Think of Guan Yin Pusa—he will help anyone, he helps all persons, all things—the whole. Is it not so? Guan Yin knows about sacrifice. Is it not Guan Yin who refuses heaven in order to help the humans and beasts? Is it not Guan Yin who becomes the young girl who gives her hands and eyes to save her father, the king? You Westerners know nothing about sacrifice," he sips his tea.

The paradox of China fills my mind. I wonder if I'm ever going to understand this country. Red Universe has somehow managed to compare Guan Yin with the Cultural Revolution and Chairman Mao, and now he's brought up the bodhisattva Vow and the Miao Shan myth to back up his theory.

I look at Jeremy and Alice: he's disgusted and frowning and she's amused and smiling. I don't know what to think. There is something particularly pragmatic about Red Universe; I can't help but like him. He has a matter-of-fact approach to situations that caused great suffering, but I don't sense a trace of cruelty in him. He's merely stating what is. All through Chinese history it has been the same: be it emperors or politicians, a small number rules the masses, deciding what's best for the group; the wise conform, the unwise perish. The current situation is no different; it just has a different name.

But when he says that Guan Yin's sacrifice is just like the people of China martyring themselves for a greater cause, I don't quite agree.

"Well, Alice, we've found someone as nutty as you. You can sit here and commiserate about how Mao is a savior. Why don't you tell him about your Mao and Jesus theory or your old man Lenin? I'm leaving. I'll see you back at the hotel," Jeremy says. He puts on his coat and hat and walks out of the teahouse. Red Universe has had the pleasure of driving two people out of his company in the past hour. He's a powerful character, his eyes twinkling as he refills his cup and lights another cigarette.

I have a great urge to leave as well. I make arrangements to meet up with Alice for dinner tomorrow and then excuse myself from the table.

"Good luck finding Guan Yin Pusa," Red Universe says. He turns and starts a conversation with Alice about the former Soviet Union. I hear the name Marx as I walk away.

The night is bitter and the street and car lights are sharp against the cold. I walk for a bit, circumambulating Tiananmen. I decide to visit the square once more in the darkness. Scurrying across the boulevard, I'm shocked to find it closed—how do you close a square?

The gates are shut and I'd have to jump the fence to get inside.

Mao's Mausoleum and the shrine to the People's Liberation Army loom in the darkness. I take out my camera and position it on a cement post to steady it for a long exposure. I focus across the dark square to the well-lit walls of the Forbidden City and Chairman Mao's illumined portrait.

Out of nowhere, two furry-collared guards arrive. They stand in front of me, blocking my view. One grabs at my camera but once they realize I'm a foreigner they allow me to take my photo. I feel the warm rush of rebellion as I take two long exposures of Tiananmen and the Forbidden City. I smile at the guards and then run back across the boulevard and disappear into the night.

On the subway, I put on my headphones and listen to *Da Bei Zhou* (*Great Mercy Dharani*) mantra. My *qigong* teacher gave me a copy of it sung by the Beijing Children's Sanskrit Choir to a Tibetan melody. It's a sweet rendition accompanied by flute and *erhu*. The *Da Bei Zhou* is said to protect all those who recite it from all kinds of perils, including violent death or death by madness or illness. And it also promises that those who recite it will be reborn in a good country to a good family and will have access to the dharma. And it is in the *Da Bei Zhou* that Guan Yin promises to forgo nirvana if anyone who recites it is not also enlightened by it.

The mantra is essentially the names of a whole bunch of gods and bodhisattvas. Saying all these names covers just about everyone you'd want to appeal to for help or understanding, including Hari, the healing god of the Hindu pantheon; Maitreya, the Buddha of the future; and of course Guan Yin.

The subway rolls, I listen to the *Da Bei Zhou* and think about Red Universe and his reference to the myth of Miao Shan. Miao Shan, the third daughter of a certain king, refused to be married off. She wanted instead to go to the White Sparrow Nunnery and become a Buddhist nun. At first her father allowed this, but in time he grew angry at her decision and had the nunnery burned down. Miao Shan escaped the fire but was caught by the royal guards who had orders to cut off her head. But the blade shattered when it struck her neck and Yama, the lord of death, came to her rescue. Miao Shan then toured the underworld and came back to earth on Putuo Island, where she apparently became enlightened.

In time, Miao Shan's father fell ill and was told that the only way he could be saved was by someone who had never felt anger sacrificing his or her own eyes and hands for him. He was told there was such a person on

Putuo Island, and he sent a messenger to ask for the sacrifice. Of course, Miao Shan agreed and chopped off her hands and plucked out her eyes and sent them to her father. When he came to pay homage after his recovery, he saw that his savior was his daughter. He was overcome with remorse and gratitude. In one story I heard, the king then had a statue honoring his daughter made and the sculptor mistakenly created a statue of Guan Yin with a thousand arms and a thousand eyes because the king was so effusive in his description of his daughter's sacrifice that the sculptor thought the king was describing Guan Yin.

As far as I know, this is only an old Chinese myth, and the connection between Miao Shan and Guan Yin came in later versions of the story. Still, the message of compassion and sacrifice is constant in both figures. But unlike Red Universe, I can't quite make the leap from Miao Shan and Guan Yin to the merits of sacrifice during the communist rule of China. And I don't like the idea of Guan Yin or Miao Shan being co-opted by a communist; from what I can tell, the "sacrifices" made during the Cultural Revolution were made by unwilling people. That sounds like the opposite of Guan Yin: she was aware when she made her vow to forgo nirvana in order to save all beings. And the same with Miao Shan: she willingly chopped off her hands and plucked out her eyes to save her father.

The subway rattles and the *Da Bei Zhou* hums in my ears. I wonder about sacrifice. Maybe what Red Universe said was right, at least regarding many Westerners today: we all talk about sacrifice, it's a common word often used lightly, but there doesn't seem to be much need for sacrifice in the West. We're told we can have everything—our whole economy is set up around it. Many of us have never lived through a war or a revolution or famine.

The *Da Bei Zhou* promises that anyone who says it will be born in a good place and have access to the dharma. According to that, many Westerners are in ideal positions for enlightenment. But what about the Chinese people: where is their access to the dharma? I think of the tea sellers—teenagers moving to the city peddle tea to support their families—and China's factory workers, living in communal apartments with eight to twelve people sharing a room, working long shifts with no time for anything but labor. It doesn't seem fair. Especially when I consider my journey here, all my leisure time, and other expats, and all their leisure time. The world feels unbalanced.

By the time I get to the hostel, I'm exhausted by the day. Being in Beijing isn't much of a holiday with all the paradoxes I'm faced with. I have a quick shower and fall into a confused sleep.

❧

Many buildings and structures of the original Summer Palace were severely damaged and burned by the French and English during the 1860s. The allies burned the palace in an attempt to persuade the Chinese to agree to new terms in the Treaty of Nanjing—specifically the clause that legalized opium. After the palace was burned, Prince Gong agreed to whatever the allies asked and the opium flowed.

In the following years, the buildings of the Summer Palace were reconstructed by the last of the Qing emperors. Then during the Cultural Revolution some parts were damaged again. But nowadays, like many historical buildings in China, the Palace has been restored and named a UNESCO World Heritage Site. Its large grounds and many halls, relatively empty of tourists today because it's winter, are beautiful amid the sunshine and fresh snow.

I was mesmerized by the Long Corridor this morning—2238 feet long with over 14,000 beams covered in traditional Chinese paintings, each step a journey to another land. I walked back and forth along it twice taking in the view, the paintings and the day.

I stood on the shore of frozen Kunming Lake and wondered at the marble boat stationed in the ice. It's designed after a two-story paddled steamer and was constructed using embezzled money. Cixi, the dowager empress of the Qing Dynasty, commissioned the boat.

She was a very powerful woman who began her career as a concubine of Xianfeng and after his death was the de facto ruler of China for over forty years. She managed to dispose of all her former emperor's successors (including her own son) and maintained power regardless of who was the appointed heir. She loathed Western ideas and seemed to look backward rather than forward. When China was attacked by sea, she was too slow in attempting to equip the navy with updated boats because she was unwilling to learn from the West. Ironically, it was during those years when the navy was failing that she had the marble boat built in Kunming Lake so she could entertain there and host parties. By most accounts, she was a despotic woman whose reign brought the end of the Qing Dynasty.

I stood looking at the Cixi's marble boat for some time. It's a beautiful piece of art, but lavishly symbolic of power gone wrong. And after my day yesterday with the communists and Maoists, I couldn't help but wonder if all power goes wrong in the end. What Red Universe said was right: China has seen one revolution after another. When something doesn't work, it's overthrown. If there's one thing that China is teaching me it is that our world is mutable.

After I turned away from the lake toward Longevity Hill, I couldn't get the absurdities of China out of my head. Dowager Empress Cixi: what is it that allows someone to control and manipulate others to the point that they can control and manipulate an entire country? And why, if they are granted that power don't they do something useful with it? She liked to have parties so she had a party boat built at the cost of preparing her navy for combat. Chairman Mao: he had nice handwriting. Only a million people perished during the Cultural Revolution and China was saved. We have to cut off the hand to save the whole. Guan Yin: she will forgo nirvana in order to save anyone who calls on her. What is real?

By the time I'd reached the steep stairs leading to Foxiang Ge (Pagoda of Buddhist Incense), I was feeling self-righteous against China's imperial past and happy that there had been a communist uprising, if only to get rid of the old dynasties and people like Cixi. I was feeling even more self-righteous against the Cultural Revolution because there's still inequality here—just look at the tea sellers from yesterday. And Guan Yin confused me: what does it really mean that she'll manifest herself for anyone who calls on her for help? And how could saying her name, or the sutra, be enough to save me?

I put on my earphones and listened to the *Da Bei Zhou* again. It calmed me as I walked up the stairs. There was a woman partway up, dressed in a green PLA jacket, thin sneakers and fluffy pink earmuffs with cats on them. She was clearing the ice off the steps and said, "Xiao xin" (be careful). I loved the paradox of the cat earmuffs with the army jacket and had to smile. She said something else and pointed up the stairs, but I didn't understand.

Foxiang Ge is eight ornate stories high, supported by red porticos under flying eaves. It is the tallest building in the Summer Palace and has a panoramic view of the surrounding countryside. I stood in the sunlight overlooking Kunming Lake and breathed in the day. I tried to appreciate the beauty of the place and let the thoughts of the communists and crazy empress Cixi fade away.

After a few minutes I felt peaceful and entered the pagoda. I turned out of the bright sun and came face to face with an enormous statue of Guan Yin. Gilded, with many arms reaching out from her sides, she was gigantic and took my breath away. I looked at her for a moment in disbelief and then I actually said, "What are you doing here?"

Guan Yin didn't respond. She just stood there, looking magnificent and remarkably spider-like with her multitude of arms, symbolic of her ability and desire to help those in need, and many heads and eyes, representing her all-seeing compassion.

I walked around the hall, held up by eight soaring pillars and admired Guan Yin. She was built during the Ming Dynasty, in 1574, when art was at a zenith and Buddhism flourished here in China. She survived the burning of the original pagoda and the communist desecration during the Cultural Revolution.

A man who worked at the Summer Palace told me that the emperors and empresses used to pray to Guan Yin in the tower. It was Cixi's nephew, Guangxu, who had the temple reconstructed after the French and British burned it. And Cixi came twice a month, on the new and full moon, to offer devotion to Guan Yin.

I walked out into the sunlight and had the distinct feeling that I'd been missing the point. The *Da Bei Zhou* promises that anyone who says it will be relieved from suffering and be reborn in good circumstances. But what if the idea of rebirth isn't literal, as in reincarnation, but figurative.

Every instant the mind can change: it can soar to insightful, appreciative heights or get bogged down in negativity and criticism. Saying the mantra, my mind takes the form of what I say—and in that instant I am in Guan Yin's presence. And in that state, of course I run into her. Just like I ran into Red Universe the Maoist after thinking about Mao all day.

I put on my earphones and listened to the *Da Bei Zhou*. I passed the ice-clearing woman in her PLA jacket and pink kitty earmuffs. She smiled at me and asked if I saw Guan Yin. I smiled back and thought, "Yes, I'm beginning to." And I continued my winter's walk through the Summer Palace, marveling at the mind's mutability.

Chapter 9

✦

Mrs. Hu and Liu Ming (Nanjing)
*A visit to Xi Xia Temple, an important day for qigong
and the fact that Guan Yin is a verb*

Biking in China requires both awareness and faith. There are designated bike lanes on most major streets. The bike lanes are as wide as a normal car lane, and all the traffic—bikes, scooters and the like—travel in the same direction. But during busy periods there can be from ten to one hundred vehicles vying for space in the lane, so you need good peripheral vision because you never know what might be coming up beside you. Sometimes it's a couple, with the boy at front and the girl sitting sidesaddle with her party sandals floating an inch above the road. There are many such couples, especially at night on warm days. Or there are the old women with their fluffy white dogs in the basket or chickens tied behind the bike, upside down.

Then there's the *mazida*—auto rickshaws. They are periodically banned in the city, probably because the drivers always break the traffic rules and travel in the wrong direction in the bike lanes. The *mazida* usually have wheelchair symbols painted on their sides. At first I thought this was because they catered to crippled people. Later I thought it was because many of the drivers are handicapped. But now I've come to think it's because they want everyone to be handicapped. I don't know how many times one has cut me off.

Other things you can encounter on the road are people transporting sludge. Each restaurant in the city has a sludge bucket outside where they put the leftovers; someone goes around and collects all the sludge at night and transports it to pig farms. I think that means that the pigs here in China are cannibals, but I try not to think too much about that. Other times you might see someone transporting scrap metal, glass, or long re-bar. There are many hazards in the bike lane, but it's exhilarating to ride in China.

A little while ago, I was crossing a bridge and the usual dividers that mark off the bike lane from regular traffic had been removed for some reason. Faced with the flow of at least fifty bikes around me, I couldn't stop and edge my way toward the curb and away from the roaring traffic that is usually safely on the other side of the lane dividers. So I kept riding with the flow.

This was fine for about thirty seconds until a bus came speeding up beside me on my left. I could see it out of the corner of my eye. But at the same time, on my right, a man with an automated three-wheel bike with a huge burlap bag filled with god knows what came up beside me. The man on the three-wheeler charged past me, but what he forgot was that his load overhung his bike considerably and was forcing me into the bus. Luckily, the bus driver saw what was happening and put on the brakes. The people behind me swerved and stopped as the man's burlap sack caught my handlebars and removed my bike from under me. I had no choice but to leap off as it was dragged up the road. The man with the auto tricycle dragged it about twenty meters up the road before dropping it. He didn't even look back; I'm certain that he didn't even know what had happened.

I have had positive biking experiences here in China. Like riding down to Fuzi Miao—the Confucius Temple—to buy plants for my balcony, then riding home with flowers and saplings spilling out of the basket and bags on the handlebars and on the back. Then there was the ride home from Purple Mountain just outside of Nanjing. There's a lake on the mountain that I like to swim in. If you go at night it's free because the park is closed. Many Chinese people think the lake is haunted, so no one is foolish enough to swim there at night except foreigners. Riding home from the lake, you don't have to pedal. The first few minutes on the cobblestone path leading down to the road is like a trip back in time. It's pitch black and the only sound is wind and the tires on the uneven stone. Once you hit the main road, it's a gradual slope past the old sentinels, past the Ming tombs and Sun Yat Sen's mausoleum, slowly gaining speed, past the old city wall and right into the heart of Nanjing.

It's about a ten-minute bike ride down busy Hanzhong Road to Mrs. Hu's flat—a journey I make almost every day since my trip to Tibet last summer, when I returned to Nanjing with dysentery. It wasn't until my diarrhea turned to yellow pus and blood that I realized how sick I was. The doctor at the hospital thought I must have drunk some water in Tibet that wasn't boiled at a temperature high enough to compensate for the elevation. He seemed quite pleased with his scientific understanding of altitude and looked around at the four student interns for nods of recognition and a further discussion on altitude and boiling point. When they finally concluded their musings, he diagnosed me with dysentery and sent me home with a variety of medicines and instructions to eat only rice porridge.

By the time Liu Ming, my *qigong* teacher and Mrs. Hu's son, came home from his trip to Sichuan, I was skin and bones and unable to meet him to practice in the park. He insisted that I go over to his mother's house for lunch every day until I regained my strength.

Although I'm no longer sick, both he and his mother insist that I come regularly.

Mrs. Hu's flat is near Xinjiakou in a gray, dusty, unfinished building. She lives on the top floor, her door decorated on the outside with a big "Fu" (fortune) symbol, two pictures of Guan Yin, and some of her calligraphy. Every wall in her apartment has many layers of poems and sutras hanging on it. She practices daily on little, thin pieces of paper and then pins her writings, often by just one corner, onto the wall. When there's a draft, the walls come alive with moving letters and crackling paper sounds—layers of mantra whispering through the flat. Many of the papers are torn in places, but she doesn't seem to mind; she just keeps writing.

Writing is literally an art in China in that it hangs on the wall as often as it's printed in books, and the practice of calligraphy is seen as a sign of personal cultivation. The act of composing a word or poem in calligraphic script is almost ritualistic, as the artists, like Mrs. Hu or Liu Ming, have undergone years of training in proper composition and speak of evoking the *qi* or nature around them when writing. It's almost like tai chi or *qigong*—they call on the "pose of phoenixes dancing, and snakes snaking," and embody them in their writing. When you look at the different types of calligraphy, it's apparent that every artist brings his or her own style to the work while still being rooted in the tradition that has been practiced and handed down for centuries.

During my first week of eating lunch at Mrs. Hu's house, she told Liu Ming to write me a large *shufa*—calligraphy. It reads, "Guan Zi Zai." She insisted that he write it because she says that his handwriting is better than hers because he studied at university and with the Daoists. He laid out the paper, stood over it, and breathed—maybe evoking the phoenixes—and then dipped his thick brush in the ink he'd prepared and wrote the calligraphy in a few deft strokes. Then he inscribed it and dated and stamped it and was finished in about two minutes. It's funny because in the West it takes artists months to complete a drawing, and *thangka* painters in Tibet can take months, too, but calligraphy only takes a few minutes. But that's a superficial understanding, because everyone knows that a good calligrapher has painted the same letters thousands of times before they start producing art like Liu Ming's.

The calligraphy is six feet tall and hangs on my wall. I look at it daily, trying to decipher its meaning. Guan Yin has two main names in Chinese: Guan Shi Yin (Observe World Sound) and Guan Zi Zai (Observe with Ease). They are translations from the two different pronunciations of her Sanskrit name *Avalokiśvara*, which can mean either Beholding Sound or Beholding God. Apparently, the names entered China at different times—with different translators. While whoever initially translated the *Heart Sutra* had an affinity to Guan Zi Zai, the name Guan Shi Yin is far more popular.

When I found out that Guan Yin was also called Guan Zi Zai, I finally understood the artistic depictions of her called the Royal Ease pose. There are pictures and statues made of her in this position. Guan Yin sits with one leg bent and a hand dangling on it while the other leg hangs over the platform on which she's sitting. Her legs are open rather wide, and she looks the way someone who is lounging in a private suite with a lover might look. The image has a quality of ease and openness that I have always liked. Now that I know her other name, the pose makes more sense. I have a picture of the Royal Ease pose on my wall beside the calligraphy that Liu Ming gave me.

This Guan Zi Zai calligraphy haunts me. I wake up with it staring at me in those big dark wispy characters in the middle of the night. My fingers write it on any surface, from steamed up bathroom mirrors to taxi windows. Everything is *Guan Zi Zai* these days.

When I visit Mrs. Hu, she often asks me, "Guan Zi Zai she shen me yise?" (What does Guan Zi Zai mean?) I try and ramble off some theory in broken Chinese or more often just laugh because I don't have any idea what it really means, other than an intellectual idea. My Mandarin is getting a lot better but it doesn't seem to matter.

It just allows me to be intellectual in two languages and Mrs. Hu insists that the meaning of the sutra is beyond language. But then she insists that saying Guan Yin or Guan Zi Zai is very important. Almost everything that comes out of Mrs. Hu's mouth is a paradox. But if I mention that, Liu Ming says, "Language is paradox!" and they both laugh.

Mrs. Hu has been a devout Buddhist her entire life, and since her husband moved to South America to set up a traditional Chinese medicine practice and Liu Ming moved to Sichuan to become a Daoist monk, she has free time to volunteer at the temple and study the scriptures. Every day at lunch we pore over the *Heart Sutra* as we eat. She loves the *Heart Sutra* and tries to explain the classical Chinese to me in modern Chinese while shoveling extra tofu onto my plate or stirring up bowls of lotus root paste. I'm beginning to understand the efficiency of classical Chinese: they often use one word where modern Chinese would require two or more. Mrs. Hu insists that most things that are worth understanding can be explained in few words. For example, Guan Yin: All I really need to do, she claims, is say Guan Yin's name.

After she says something like that, Liu Ming will usually pipe up and tell me to stop thinking so much and to not bother reading scriptures and to practice *qigong* instead. He's always going on about how Guan Yin (or Guan Zi Zai) is an excellent *qigong* practitioner.

He says that Buddhists think too much. Then Mrs. Hu will say that Daoists have no respect for scriptures. And Liu Ming will retort with something like, "Daoists respect everything," and quote Zhuangzi, saying it's better to be a regular turtle living by the riverside dragging his tail in the mud than a dead turtle's shell used for divination. To which she'll smile and say, "See, no respect."

Daoism and Buddhism have many similarities, but they also have a long-standing rivalry here in China. Any Chinese person will tell you that no matter how long it has been here, Buddhism is still an imported religion, whereas Daoism is Chinese and dates back to the fourth century BCE.

During Buddhism's nearly 2000 years here, the two philosophies have influenced each other considerably, but there have been notable disagreements over the ages, particularly when Buddhism managed to wiggle its way into the palaces and Buddhist teachers began to have sway over emperors. Or when Buddhist monasteries were exempt from taxation and grew in wealth.

In his *Journey to the West*, Wu Chengen pokes fun at the Daoists by always making them the bad guys. Not as bad as the demons, but corrupt. In one chapter, Monkey King plays a trick on the Daoist priests at a temple by manifesting as one of their gods. They make him offerings on the altar; Monkey pees in the offering bowls when they're not looking and then bids them to drink it. But in other chapters, Monkey gets in hot water with some Daoist priests after destroying their immortality tree and has to get Guan Yin to come all the way from Putuo Island to save him from their wrath.

I've always liked Daoist philosophy and, like many Chinese laypeople, I sometimes mix Chinese Buddhist philosophy with Daoism.

Today Mrs. Hu has arranged for Liu Ming, Xiao Song, and me to travel out to Qi Xia Temple to meet her Buddhist teacher.

Xiao Song is a well-dressed Taiwanese traditional Chinese medical student who also practices *qigong* with Liu Ming. We get along really well. During my bout with dysentery, he and Liu Ming did all sorts of strange bloodletting, cupping, moxa burning and acupuncture injections with hypodermic needles on me. Xiao Song is a disciple of Sri Sri Ravi Shankar and spends time at his ashram in India. That said, he seems to be at ease in just about any spiritual environment and has a great love for Buddhism, Daoism, Christianity, and whatever else comes his way. He often gasps audibly in wonder at any hint of spiritual insight. He's very eager to come to the temple and meet Shifu.

It's been over a year since I visited Qi Xia Temple, its tall, yellow walls welcoming as we approach and the lush mountain reaching above it, speckled with the 1000 Buddha Caves damaged during the Cultural Revolution. Last year the smashed statues disturbed me. Today I'm not interested in statues—smashed or not. I keep my gaze in front of me as we enter a corridor and courtyard into the more private monks' quarters. Liu Ming tells me to think of some questions to ask Shifu. I try and think of some as we peek through the ornate wooden carvings into the window where Shifu and his attendants are about to lunch.

Shifu is the head abbot of the temple and one of China's foremost Chan (Zen) Buddhism teachers. He's pretty old, wearing a gray monk suit and a woolly winter hat similar to mine. I can see from his eye movements that he likes my hat as much as I like his. Although we've already eaten, he and his assistants insist that we have some lunch. It's a modest spread of vegetables, tofu and rice. Once one of the serving plates is empty, a little warm water is poured on it, swished with chopsticks and drunk. Not a grain of rice is wasted. Although it's a cold winter's day and the room is drafty with stone floors, there is warmth to the atmosphere.

"You and South Sea Guan Yin have predestiny. We also have predestiny," says Shifu, ensuring that I scrape the last grain of rice from my lunch bowl. His voice is one of those raspy-creaky old-man voices that lends itself well to the tones of his regional dialect, making him almost unintelligible to everyone except the elderly female assistant who translates his dialect into a more standard Chinese. I wonder how Shifu can tell by just looking at me that I have predestiny with South Sea Guan Yin?

South Sea Guan Yin is the white-robed Guan Yin often depicted with a willow branch and a vase full of compassionate nectar and seated on a lotus with a full moon overhead. In the centuries it took for her cult to travel across China from India and Tibet, Guan Yin acquired various iconographical depictions based on sutras, folk tales, and stories of devotees. South Sea Guan Yin is a localized representation of some of the facets of her character originally associated with Putuo Island off the coast of Ningbo. South Sea Guan Yin supposedly resides on the island, near the Purple Bamboo Grove and by the Cave of Tidal Sound, where she perceives the world's suffering and penetrates the meaning of sound all day long.

In the dreams and visualizations I have had of Guan Yin, I often see her robed in white, often by the sea, with the moon and a small house. The only variation I have is that she's usually about ten feet tall, with enormous eyes and long hands and fingernails. It was on the belief in that image that I came to China. But I've lately given up on images, with the exception of Pocket Guan Yin, whom I thought I had given away last month but who has reappeared in my life. I had put her in Matt's bag when he was leaving for Australia, but when I returned home from dropping him at the airport I found Guan Yin on my bed with a tiny note saying, "You might want to lose me, but I don't want to lose you."

Xiao Song tells Shifu that a book publisher has asked me to write a book on Guan Yin based on some articles I've published. Shifu smiles.

"You have affinity with Guan Yin," he says, "and the book is already written." There is a long pause and then he smiles. Xiao Song gasps enthusiastically and Liu Ming smiles. All the disciples smile and whisper.

I finish drinking the water used to rinse my lunch bowl clean, to the approval of Shifu and the woman overseeing the meal. I try to formulate a question to ask about Guan Yin but nothing comes to mind. I feel questioned out. We all sit silently for a while until one of the young monks gets up and leaves the room. He returns with a copy of the *Heart Sutra* and a poster with eighty-four incarnations of Guan Yin painted on it.

"Guan Yin has eighty-four forms," he announces with a big grin. He hands me the poster and sutra. Liu Ming smiles at me and then looks out the window.

"Ah," I say, holding the poster. The depictions are line drawings in full color. I let my eyes pass over the various images of her. I recognize many of them, including Water Moon and South Sea Guan Yin. There's even a drawing of Putuo Island, as if to say the entire island is Guan Yin. For some reason, I'm more interested in the texture of the poster than the representations of her. I run my hands over the laminate and let the poster roll back into a tight tube on my lap.

"Do you believe what he says?" Shifu asks me.

"I thought she had more forms than that," I answer.

The four older ladies lean across the huge round table whispering to each other.

"She has countless forms!" Shifu says. "She is in everything. She is like a wave of the sea. Remember that. You know Guan Yin, you are close to her, I can see. But remember what Hui Neng says: 'Ci bei jiu shi Guan Yin'—Compassion and mercy are Guan Yin."

Hui Neng was the founder of Chan Buddhism. He wrote a famous sutra—the *Sutra of Hui Neng*—in which he says things such as, "Use *prajna* for witnessing and take an attitude of neither indifference nor attachment toward all things." He would also say not to rely on scriptural authority, but rather make use of inner wisdom by constant practice of contemplation and observation. That is probably what Guan Zi Zai is doing in the *Heart Sutra*—she is, after all, the master perceiver.

Shifu points to the *Heart Sutra*. "That is the essence of Guan Yin," he says. The disciples all nod. "Say her name," he says, "and you will understand."

"I have been saying her name," I say.

"Keep saying it," he says.

"Guan Zi Zai," I say.

I gather up the *Heart Sutra* and the poster and thank Shifu again. The four old ladies rush over to me and shake my hand saying, "Amituo Fo." One of them says something about Qingtu—or Pure Land, referring to Amitabha's Buddha land where devotees are reborn. But I don't understand what the old lady is getting at.

Shifu calls to me as I walk toward the door, "Remember, it's not suffering that needs to be transcended—it's you!" He laughs. We're ushered out into the courtyard.

We stroll toward the main square past devotees burning bright pink incense and bowing to the four directions. I repeat Guan Zi Zai silently. I think of Pure Land—the land of Amitabha and Guan Yin. This idea of Pure Land always confused me because I like Guan Yin. I see her, I dream about her and her house, but I don't believe in Pure Land. I never have. I've never believed in netherworlds. The reason I came to China is because I thought she was in this world. And it is nauseating to think of myself living another life in a netherworld.

I have to assume that Pure Land is a symbolic representation of a pure state of mind. But if that's the case, why speak of Pure Land or of transcendence? Why not call it Pure Mind and stop confusing everyone?

As we reach the gate of the monastery, Liu Ming grabs the Guan Yin poster out of my hand. He knocks me on the head with it. It makes a dull, hollow thud. He laughs. I stop thinking about Pure Land and hail us a cab.

The cab whisks us through the thick green countryside toward the gray city. I sit in the front seat beside the driver as he smokes. The car is terribly cold because he has the window down, not because he's smoking but so that he can spit periodically. He has an awful cough. From what I'm told, the Chinese government owns the cigarette companies and that's why there's such a push to smoke here and no warnings about possible threats to health.

The following day at lunch, I took my usual seat at Mrs. Hu's, in the misplaced captain's chair in the corner of the dining room (which is also the hallway), and perused the recent additions to her calligraphy. Like many Chinese people, Mrs. Hu insists on keeping the windows open, even in the winter. There was more of a gale than a draft in the apartment, and most of her calligraphy fluttered and threatened to tear from the wall. This didn't seem to faze her.

Lunch was hot pot. The wok sat in the center of the table over a propane flame. Beside it were piles of uncooked meat, a couple of fish heads, and many kinds of vegetables. Hot pots generally make me nervous because when I stick my chopsticks into the bubbling brew, I never know what I'm going to pull out. The odds are fairly good that it will be meat of some sort, and I'm supposed to be a vegetarian.

That said, in recent months, Liu Ming has insisted that I eat some meat. He says that the "karma" of China is very strong because of what has happened here during the Cultural Revolution and I need to fortify myself as much as possible. So, after being a vegetarian since the age of five, I've started to eat a bit of pork and chicken. I don't like it.

Mrs. Hu asked us about our trip to the monastery. I explained everything and then I brought up that thing that Shifu said to me about transcendence. I asked her why Buddhists always speak of transcendence.

"Who was speaking about transcendence?" she asked.

"Shifu. He said that it's not suffering that needs to be transcended—it's me."

She scraped some vegetables and meat into the hot pot and they began to roll and boil, dark forms in the froth. "It sounds like he meant that it is your *idea* of transcendence that needs to be transcended—not suffering," she said.

But I wouldn't give up. I thought about the sketch that Mrs. Hu drew for me when she was trying to illustrate the mantra at the end of the *Heart Sutra*: "gate gate paragate parasamgate bodhi svaha"—"gone, gone, gone way beyond to the other shore." She took one of her thick calligraphy pens and drew a little picture of the sea with an arrow from one side pointing to Guan Yin on the other, meaning that Guan Yin had crossed the ocean of *samsara* and lived on the other shore. When I saw the picture I had a similar reaction as I had when I thought about Shifu's comment: What is the point of talking about going to some other shore when earlier in the sutra Guan Yin realizes that matter is void?

"In the sutra, Guan Zi Zai perceives the emptiness of all things, including feelings, perceptions, formations, consciousness. So of course she is free and fearless. But doesn't that mean that there is no transcendence? Isn't that how the bodhisattvas manage to stay in our world? They know there's nowhere to go—this is the void!" I announced.

The hot pot bubbled and spat on the table. Mrs. Hu laughed. "Don't talk about the void with your tongue: practice it with your body and senses and your mind.

Too many people talk about vacuity with their tongues. Too many talk about compassion with their tongues and they don't know either. Definitely it is your mind that needs transcending, not suffering. Practice your *qigong* and say her name," she said.

So I've been saying *Guan Zi Zai* and practicing *qigong* every afternoon with Liu Ming and Xiao Song for the past month. We've been practicing *Zhuang Huai Dan*—a nine-part form of *qigong* that aids concentration and strengthens *dantian*—the center of the body. Liu Ming says that if you practice these nine moves, you don't need to practice anything else—that they contain the essence of *qigong* and tai chi. The poses have great names: "Lifting the pearl from the bottom of the sea" and other such poetic things. Practicing the form always makes me feel as tall as the sky, as wide as the earth and as deep as the sea.

We alternate between this form and something Liu Ming calls "Da Hai," or Great Sea. We stand in the park in an open posture and wait until the *qi* moves us. If it does, we move into another pose—quite spontaneously. If the *qi* doesn't move us we remain still. To observe us, you might think we were doing a kind of slow improvised dance. To practice, it feels like we're floating in a sea of *qi*, bobbing and being held afloat by the ebb and flow of waves.

Liu Ming is also teaching me about the *Nong Li*—China's agricultural calendar. The *Nong Li* has 24 *Jie Qi*, or seasons. The *Jie* mark the beginning of the month and the *Qi* mark the middle of the month and have names such as "Awakening the Insects," "White Dew" and "Clear Brightness." Chinese New Year, or Spring Festival, falls on the first of the *Jie*, but each *Jie* or *Qi* has its own significance. The *Nong Li* is based on the degree of the sun, so the seasons can change on different dates each year.

To make things more cyclical, the twenty-four hours of the day can be broken down into seasons—which also correspond to the twenty-four-season calendar. For example, from 11:00 p.m. to 1:00 a.m. on a given day is related to the winter solstice in the Chinese calendar—the darkest time or the year, and the darkest time of the day—and the most "yin" time as well.

In some *qigong* schools, the hour to practice *qigong* changes depending on the season. Some say it is wise to practice at the same time of day as the season you are in. Others insist that it's good to practice when there is more yang, or sun, because humans are not naturally nocturnal and need the sun.

Today between 7:00 p.m. and 9:00 p.m. the season changes to *Da Han*—Great Cold. And Liu Ming insists that *Da Han* is an important time. So we are to practice *qigong* all afternoon to get ready for tonight.

It was based on the *Nong Li* that Liu Ming decided that I should study *qigong* in the first place. I chanced upon him at my friend's place one night when he was there doing Ba Gua, a sort of astrology based on the date and time of birth which is related to the *Nong Li*. I wasn't interested in getting mine done but he insisted, and it revealed that I would be a "suitable" practitioner of *qigong*. He said that if I hadn't been sitting in front of him, he would have thought that he was looking at a Ba Gua reading for a Buddhist nun with a weak stomach. I don't know how he figured that out by looking at my birth time, but he was confident in his reading. Based on the reading he insisted that I practice *qigong*. I wasn't looking for instruction but I agreed to come and meet him the next day. I am his only female student and his only Western student. The rest are wiry young guys who are mainly interested in Liu Ming's tai chi and sword displays. Xiao Song and I are the only ones learning *qigong*.

We stand between the two tall gingko trees facing the pale sun. I forgot my mitts. Liu Ming gives me a dirty look and says I'd better get the *qi* moving to warm myself up. It doesn't take long for my hands to tingle with *qi*.

"Guan Zi Zai," I say quietly to myself.

Liu Ming has said that Guan Yin or Guan Zi Zai is an excellent *qigong* practitioner because she practices *wuwei*. *Wuwei*—nonaction—is the Daoist way of describing a state of ease and oneness and being with the flow of nature. *Wuwei* is similar to *zizai*: when we are at one with the Dao, everything we do is *wuwei*.

I want more clarification and ask Liu Ming, "If I am *zizai*—at ease—everything I do is like Guan Zi Zai or Guan Yin, right?"

He doesn't answer. I put my tongue against my palate to complete the circuit in the body—apparently most *qi* leaks out between your legs or your mouth, a point that Liu Ming often repeats. In Daoist practice, there is an emphasis on keeping the circuit closed, so you are to contract your perineum and keep your tongue on your palate.

I lower my eyes gently and watch my breath. My arms and torso feel like they're suspended from above. My legs, connected with the ground, feel like they are drawing energy from below. With each inhalation the brightness grows; with each exhalation the waves lengthen and draw me out until I feel as wide as the sea and as tall as the sky. My whole body begins moving with the *qi*, the same way you would move in a big lake with the lilt of waves and the buoyancy of water.

The three of us stand for a long time in an open position, visualizing light and *qi* as the sky dims and the air grows cold. At the end of the session, Liu Ming reminds us to practice at home at exactly 7:00 p.m. so that we can feel the changing of the season.

I float home along Hanzhong Road, in the usual altered state that *qigong* invokes. I push my bike beside me and listen to my breath washing like the ebb and flow of the tide. It's rush hour and there is a lot of movement and sound in the city. Many small shops bustle with customers and lights and music. Many small restaurants prepare dinner, their various smells wafting out onto the street.

In front of the Bank of China, my feet on the dirty red-and-white sidewalk with a stream of bicycles flowing by, I begin to understand. *Guan Zi Zai.* The thought blows in like a breeze through my mind. I can feel my perception changing. I hear the weight of the words revealing themselves: *Guan Zi Zai* is a verb.

Her name is a directive: to observe/perceive with ease, to observe/perceive the sounds of the world. She's not a being—she's a way of being. In saying her name I've been telling myself to do this over and over again but not listening to the message. I've been looking all over China for a noun and ignoring the verb. No wonder Shifu told me to keep saying her name.

Many thoughts assemble themselves: to be at ease and to observe within is to be "Guan Zi Zai." To observe the sounds of the world, and compassionately, is to be "Guan Shi Yin." Her names are the means of perceiving existence—witnessing the world. When I "Guan Zi Zai," or observe my actions and thoughts and sense perceptions with ease, I know that although everything in the world rises and falls, that which perceives them does not.

I hear my breath coming and going, I feel my breath coming and going, I see my breath coming and going, I taste my breath coming and going, I smell my breath coming and going. So what is it that perceives?

I turn into my laneway and drift along the broken sidewalk beside the tall wall of the Christian center. The gray buildings and the gray sky up ahead are almost in-distinguishable, fusing before me. Far down the street, the blind lady with the bell begins to resound. I often listen to her make her way past my apartment and then turn up Ci Bei—Compassion and Mercy Street—and ting out of earshot. I'm usually six stories up, listening from a height. But today I will meet her head on. She's timeless in her blue-gray revolutionary suit and sewn up eyes. Although she's blind, I get a sense that she has seen quite a bit. Her steps are small but deliberate as she plots her way through a world without sight, her chimes growing sharper as she approaches.

I'm not entirely sure what the point of her bell is—to notify people of her presence? No one seems to hear it—cars too wide for the lane and crazy *mazida* rattle and honk as they tear past her. Maybe she uses the bell to clear her mind or keep time amid all the other noises of Nanjing. I step into the lane to give her room on the sidewalk. She turns her head and faces me, although I'm not sure how she knows I'm here. I smile at the blind lady and she tings her bell—the sound piercing and then warm as it ripples through me.

The apartment is dark and my roommates are out. I sit in silence in front of my Guan Yin statue. I'm warm all over and very relaxed. My mind feels clear, but I'm aware of just how long I have been searching for Guan Yin, and how funny it is that I'd never even thought of the fact that her name is a verb.

At 7:00 p.m. I stand up, as Liu Ming said, and practice *qigong* once more. I take an open posture and wait. I don't know how much time passes before an intense breath rushes through me, followed by a humming silence. It feels like there is a strong wind in the apartment, or a wave flooding through the place.

The season has changed. All the furniture, the window, the buildings outside and I all float together in the sea of *qi*. I feel connected with everything and calmly detached at the same time.

Chapter 10

❧

Guan Yin's Island (Putuo Shan)
SARS scare in China and a trip
to Guan Yin's island in the East China Sea

The battle against SARS (severe acute respiratory syndrome) is in full force—makeshift hospitals are going up in Beijing and other major centers overnight, housing thousands of quarantined people. It took about a month of pressure from the World Health Organization and other countries, such as Canada, that have incidences of the virus for the Chinese government to admit that SARS is a problem and that it originated here in China. But it has suddenly been deemed a national priority, and overnight propaganda posters appeared plastered all over the city. Everyone is talking about how to win the war against SARS. Walking down the street is like a trip to a nuclear fallout city: everyone wears white masks or bandanas when they have to enter public places. I have noticed that the masks have inhibited but not prevented nose-picking and gobbing and other pastimes, so it's questionable whether they serve any purpose besides making everyone look funny. But even if the masks don't work, another tactic has surfaced—vinegar is being boiled everywhere because SARS apparently doesn't like the smell.

So far there are seven cases of SARS in Nanjing and a thousand people in quarantine. The First of May holiday has been postponed across the country, and Chinese citizens are not allowed to exit or enter cities: everyone is to stay put to prevent further infection. All universities are closed for the next two weeks—students living on campus are not permitted to leave, and those of us living off campus are not allowed to enter. The factory workers are allowed to travel only from their near-factory housing to their workplaces. The street vendors have been rounded up, the internet bars closed. My recording job at the provincial studio has also stopped, so I've been in limbo for the past few days, left to marvel at the efficiency of the Chinese government's control over its citizens.

For May holiday, the entire country is granted five days off to travel. Usually, hundreds of millions of people do exactly this, and consequently all the tourist spots are so packed, I don't know how people enjoy themselves. I've often wondered why they don't stagger the holidays. But I suppose it's the same line of thinking that has put all of China in the same time zone. To see that the government also has the power to stop a countrywide holiday, indeed to stop travel for two weeks, is both wondrous and alarming to me.

I've found the restrictions disorienting. It's strange to live in a foreign city and have all of my regular haunts closed, my classes cancelled, and my jobs postponed for two weeks. I'd been feeling somewhat aimless until yesterday. I was riding my bike down the street past a stream of white masked Chinese cyclists when it dawned on me: I'm not Chinese; I'm a foreigner. I'm allowed to travel. And where does one travel when everyone else in China is quarantined? Guan Yin's home, the island of Putuo!

Early morning is always soft and quiet, with bicycles creaking and breakfast stalls set up in laneways. But since the SARS scare hit Nanjing, all of my favorite breakfast stands have been outlawed. And to make things worse, there was a tragedy at a breakfast stall outside of the city last week. The facts are unclear because the Chinese press isn't covering the event, but apparently ninety people were poisoned at a breakfast stand somewhere in the suburbs. Supposedly a man who used to work at the stand was jealous of the owner and sought to win over customers by making them sick from eating at his rival's stand. He put rat poisoning—strychnine—into his former boss's food. Upon eating their breakfasts, many people started vomiting blood and dying on the street. The man was arrested, convicted, and sentenced to death within a couple of days. Apparently he wasn't given the luxury of the new Chinese "death vans," which arrive at the court and give lethal injections. He was treated to the old standby and shot.

So between SARS and this recent event, it's been hard to find street breakfast in the past few weeks. But there are some intrepid vendors who hide in dark laneways offering my favorite treat—*youtiao*, a kind of donut wrapped in a fine crepe with savory vegetables, cooked over a coal fire. I seek them out and then head to meet Tino.

Tino is one of a group of vegetarians I've been eating lunch with every day for the past month. We pay a Chinese woman to shop and cook for us and she makes delicious vegetarian faux meat dishes, rice and fresh veggies. We all meet at a Belgian student's house and eat together with the cook. Apart from me, everyone at the flat is a member of a spiritual organization headed by world-famous Master Qinghai. Master Qinghai is Vietnamese by birth but has become very popular in Taiwan and other parts of Asia, including China. Her main meditation technique is called Guan Yin (light and sound rather than Guan Yin as observing sound). All of Master Qinghai's disciples are vegetarians and although I'm not a follower of her work, I get along well with the group. Tino is the most recent addition to the followers. He recently arrived in China after an extended stay at Osho's ashram in Puna. He might be called a seeker, or maybe he's found what he was looking for with Master Qinghai. Regardless, he's in China on holiday and is eager to accompany me to Putuo Island.

The train car from Nanjing to Ningbo is empty besides us. After being in the country for almost two years and getting used to being squeezed onto public transport, it's almost eerie. Tino and I sit sprawled across three seats each and take in the scenery as we move southeast. The Yangzi Delta is lush green, spotted with occasional houses and villages, fish farms and local plastic bag dumps. It seems that some of the peasants either don't care that the refuse is close to their fish and vegetable farms, clearly contaminating them, or else they have nowhere else to dump their plastic bags and garbage and are trying to at least consolidate it.

After the train ride and a series of city buses to the coast, we finally make it to the ferry port. We have to wait until morning for a ferry that will take us to an island near Putuo. We wander the coastal town at dusk. SARS doesn't seem to be a major scare here—there are lots of people on the street eating in the soft breeze. Tino and

I buy some cheap street fare, take in the night air and then return to our hotel.

The following morning the port is empty except for a few Chinese tourists, several government workers, and a woman dressed in white from head to toe. She points an electric gun at my head and takes my temperature. It's low enough that I don't have SARS; she signs a yellow card stating so. Tino is allowed through as well. We board the near-empty ferry and watch as we pull away from the mainland and carve our way through misty-mountained islands into the East China Sea.

The boat ports at another empty dock. We have to take a bus for twenty minutes to the other side of the island and then find a ferry that will take us to Putuo. A tiny man with a lazy eye sits in front of a twenty-five-foot boat with a large bow. I tell him that we want to go to Putuo. He smiles and says that Putuo is closed—all the shops, all the bars—and that there's nothing to do or see but *ziran*—scenery. He lights a cigarette and looks out at the sea, ignoring us. I look at the sea and consider swimming. The dim water and rolling waves laugh back at me. Tino suggests that we wait. We sit down on the dock beside the small ferryman, and I tell him that we're not interested in bars and shops—that we came to see Guan Yin.

His face softens and he says that Putuo is Guan Yin's special place and where she lives—it's the most beautiful place. He says that there are no tour groups but the island is still open and of course he will take us. Once we're out at sea, I'm grateful for how large the boat's bow is—waves roll right over it as we rise and fall. I watch the small ferryman and think of all the myths about sailors and pilgrims who, when coming into trouble on the waters of the East China Sea, called on Guan Yin for help. Guan Yin isn't the kind of bodhisattva that just sits around pontificating about the sutras from her lotus throne—she comes to those who call, those in need. I hope she's watching over us on this ride. After all, it would be a shame, after all this time in China, for me to drown within a couple of kilometers of Putuo. We dock unscathed. The ferryman wishes us luck finding a place to sleep and floats away.

Putuo is lush—bamboo whispering, elephant ears collecting dew, moss-covered rocks peaking out from behind palms. The entire island is only 8.3 kilometers long. It is mountainous, but there is no spot on the mountain that is farther than a kilometer from the sea—the best of both worlds. The Purple Bamboo Grove, Cave of Tidal Sound, Guan Yin Leap, and thirty-meter Guan Yin are some of the attractions of the island.

It's said that the island was originally Daoist, but the Buddhists took over during the Tang Dynasty (618–907) and the government funded its rise as a Buddhist pilgrimage site during other dynasties. In 847, an Indian Buddhist monk came here to cultivate his "Buddha nature" and apparently heard the scriptures delivered by Guan Yin herself.

In 916, the Japanese monk Huie, while attempting to transport a statue of Guan Yin from China to Japan, fell into trouble on the stormy sea and called on Guan Yin for help. The story goes that she brought him safely to Putuo. He built a hall to enshrine the statue and named it "Don't Want to Leave" hall. Over the centuries, the island became very well known as Guan Yin's special home. I'm not sure when it became known as Putuo, but the name comes from the *Huayan Jing—the Flower Garland Sutra*—where Guan Yin's home, Potoloka, is described as a mountain abode at the end of the ocean.

At one point, Putuo is said to have held as many as 200 monasteries. And as with all successive dynasties in China, these monasteries flourished for a time and then waned. Then, of course, during the Cultural Revolution, most of the remaining monasteries were destroyed. Nowadays only a handful of monasteries and nunneries remain, but some are under construction once again. This is the way things are in China—rising and falling and rising once more in a different form, in a different dynasty. It's only those of us who are caught up in our own short lifetimes who think things are permanent— or not permanent.

One side of the island is a fish farm; there's a navy port as well. But if the main port was any indication, it's clear that the island's latest incarnation is as a tourist destination: it has docks that accommodate enormous boats and welcomes hundreds of thousands of tourists every year. When I first came to China, I didn't want to visit Putuo because I was disheartened that it had been destroyed during the Cultural Revolution, and worse, has recently become a tourist trap. I couldn't stand the idea that Guan Yin's mythical island was an amusement park with karaoke bars and overrun with noisy tour groups. Besides, I was fixated on Guan Yin's form and would likely have been overwhelmed in the presence of all the Guan Yin statues.

I had heard of Guan Yin Leap—a rocky precipice where Guan Yin apparently left her footprint while leaping to a nearby island. It is said that many tourists have seen visions of Guan Yin there and leaped to their deaths trying to reach her, or mutilated themselves in offering. I had been worried that I might do something like that in a moment of Guan Yin ecstasy. On top of that, I was convinced that the house I'd seen in dreams and meditations was somewhere on this island—and I knew I would be devastated if I couldn't find it. So, like someone caught in an illusion, instead of breaking it, I prolonged it because it was more comfortable.

But that was before I learned that Guan Yin, or Guan Zi Zai, is a way of being rather than a physical being and doesn't necessarily differentiate between monasteries and karaoke bars and doesn't live in a specific place. So I feel like I can finally visit here because I don't have any expectations of finding Guan Yin or her house. Tino and I wander on a stone path into the center of the island, meeting no one, hearing only rustling leaves in the gingko trees and feeling the warm sun. Rounding a bend, we run into a woman, hunched over by the side of the road, surrounded by boxes and statues—Guan Yin statues, at least thirty of them, identical, sprawled out half-wrapped in packing paper and Styrofoam. We pause to admire them—white porcelain with hand-painted faces and flowers. The woman wants me to buy one. I smile and keep walking, impressed with my own detachment toward Guan Yin's form!

The downtown square of Putuo surrounds a large pond with stone bridges and immense trees. There's a quietude and ease to the place, magnified by the fact that there are no tour groups. Walls inscribed with enormous calligraphy read "Namo Guan Shi Yin Pusa" and "Namo Guan Zi Zai Pusa." Nuns and monks in gray-blue suits mill about giggling and clowning around. And there are a few locals, sitting on a stone wall smoking and smiling. They laugh at us and tell us that we're going to have a hard time finding a place to eat and sleep—the island is closed. I tell them that Guan Yin will help us and they laugh some more.

They're right. All the hotels are closed and there's no sign of any food. We wander up an old street lined with gray garage doors—all closed. I imagine that they are shops and restaurants that are normally teeming with tourists at this time of the year. I pause beside the large fountain and wonder for a moment if this isn't perfect—I finally make it to Guan Yin's island and it's closed. We take another walk through the square and meet a small woman dressed in a tan suit. She asks me if we need a place to stay. I tell her that we do and that we also need something to eat. She brings us to her uncle's house—a small damp place just off the main street—and says that we can stay in their spare room for ten yuan a night. She assures us that some shops are open, as well as a vegetarian restaurant, because there are some tourists here from Taiwan and other countries. And, of course, all the monasteries and nunneries are open.

Morning in Putuo is soft and sweet. After a breakfast of rice porridge, pickles and steamed vegetable buns Tino and I decided to split up. I wandered toward Raining Dharma Temple, a splendid structure built in the Tang Dynasty with bright-colored buildings, pristine gardens and silence. I didn't have any great inclination to visit the various halls, so I closed my eyes and sat outside the main hall and listened to the monks chanting Namo Amitabha to the roll of a fish-shaped woodblock and cymbals. I sat for about half an hour, absorbed the mantra and waited for Xiao Hesheng.

Xiao Hesheng—little monk—is the name I gave the monk I met last night in the bookstore—one of the only shops open. He stood by the wall in his blue-gray monk's suit, knickers, long socks, and sandals reading a book about Chairman Mao. I asked him why he, a monk, was reading about Mao, and he asked me why I, a non-monk, wasn't reading about Mao. I didn't have an answer and we laughed and became friends. Xiao Hesheng's been a monk for only ten months. He just moved to Putuo from the south, where he was a businessman. His front teeth are gold-rimmed, and something about his general air made me tell him that if he wasn't wearing a monk's uniform I wouldn't have believed that he was a monk. He told me that that's why he has to wear his uniform.

Xiao Hesheng may not be the most dutiful monk but he's a good tour guide, ensuring that I see all the wonders of the island. To begin with, he took me through a couple of temples and we burned large pink and yellow sticks of incense to every deity we came across. Then he showed me an enormous camphor tree and explained that it's an incarnation of Guan Yin: "Guan Yin is everywhere on Putuo," he said.

But because I love Guan Yin, he insisted that I see the thirty-meter statue of her. I wasn't sure whether I wanted to see a thirty-meter statue of Guan Yin first thing in the morning, concerned that the sheer size of it might be too much for me. After all, I only recently overcame my fixation on her form.

I reminded him that he had told me that everything on the island is Guan Yin—so we didn't need to visit the statue. We could instead have a break from touring and I could go to the sea. But before I finished my sentence he had crossed his arms. I knew then that we were going to have an argument and that I was going to lose. In all of my time in China, I've never won an argument with a Chinese person. They have a way of being fundamentally right, even in the face of reason.

He said, "Ni meiyou limao"—"You have no manners." And insisted that it would be rude for me to come all the way to Putuo and not pay my respects to South Sea Guan Yin.

Before I knew it, I stood before thirty-meter South Sea Guan Yin—the vibrant blue sky framing her dark bronze form. She was holding a wheel, symbolic of her help for fishermen. There was no one around except for Xiao Hesheng and me. He bowed. I bowed. He wandered off somewhere and I was left alone before her enormous form. Unsure of what to do, I took my Pocket Guan Yin out of my pocket and held her in front of my face before the enormous statue. If I held Pocket Guan Yin close enough to my eye, she was taller than the thirty-meter statue. I laughed. Xiao Hesheng came back and asked me what I was laughing at. I showed him my optical illusion. He thought it was splendid and laughed too.

We walked, and I thought about how many people must love Guan Yin as much as I do for there to be such a statue celebrating her on an island dedicated to her. I thought of all the devotees in China, Taiwan and other Asian countries and calculated that she might be the most prayed to form in our world. And considering she isn't confined to a specific form, she might be the most prayed to non-form as well.

During lunch I told Xiao Hesheng about my visions of Guan Yin and her house by the sea and my reason for coming to China. He listened attentively to my still-faltering Mandarin and at the end of my explanation decided that I must certainly have *yuanfen* with Guan Yin and that she must have blessed me to let me come to Putuo. I explained to him that I know that she isn't a physical being, and that her house is probably a symbolic place inside of myself rather than a physical place on Putuo. I explained that I know that she's a verb, not a noun.

He didn't agree. He said decidedly that she was a verb but that she was also a noun, and he asked me how I knew that her house wasn't on the island. I said I didn't know.

⌘

Xiao Hesheng wants to take Tino and me to the beach. He says it's a good place to watch the sunset and listen to the crashing waves. We ask him why he doesn't have monk duties to do at his monastery but he doesn't respond. He gives us each a preserved plum to eat instead. It's salty and sour, a taste I've grown accustomed to in China. Tino makes a face at the taste. I suck on the pit as Xiao Hesheng leads us to the sea. The one road that runs north–south along the island is empty, the greenery buzzing in the late afternoon heat.

The sand is soft and white on the beach, warm on my bare feet. There's a swing and Xiao Hesheng insists that Tino push him on it. They look ridiculous—a tiny Chinese monk being pushed on a swing by a large blond man. I walk ahead. The coast is clear except for scurrying crabs.

I pick up a stick on the shore and practice writing Chinese characters in the sand. The waves creep up behind me, lapping my feet. I write my name and then I write the *Heart Sutra* in the sand. Waves edge toward my efforts, washing them away. This is the way it ought to be—sutras in the sand disappearing in the ocean. I play the sutra sand-washing game for a while and grow relaxed. Relaxed with the reality that I can't write more than a few characters before the waves wash it away. It makes me wonder what the point of striving is. No wonder they call Guan Yin *Guan Zi Zai*—the one who is at ease: what is there to strive for? Everything, even her name as I write it, is being washed in the sea.

I'm not sure what it is that causes me to pause and look down the coast. Or what it is that has prevented me from seeing what sits on the precipice at the end of Thousand Step Beach when we first came down here. But as clear as day, soaring over the sea at the end of the beach, is a building I've seen before. I recognize it. I recognize the gazebo below it and the rock that jets out from the ocean in front of the gazebo. I've drawn it many times in journals and letters describing my search for Guan Yin. I'm shocked and not at all surprised to see it. I tell Xiao Hesheng that I've seen the building before, in meditation and in dreams. I stood below it by the gazebo watching the sea and the fish with a friend of mine in a dream. I'm calm as I explain all of this, and I have the distinct feeling that the building is empty. Xiao Hesheng says that it is empty—but that it has a nice garden. He offers to take me there. I decline and suggest that we walk back into town.

In the main square, Xiao Hesheng, Tino and I run into another monk who is sitting on a stone wall chatting with a nun. He wears glasses and has bushy eyebrows. She's young, with a very round face and chubby cheeks. They both wear the same gray-knickered outfit as Xiao Hesheng and sandals with socks on. Xiao Hesheng introduces us and tells the monk and nun about my journey from Canada all the way to Putuo looking for Guan Yin. The monk seems to think that's a noble pursuit and starts going on about how Guan Yin lives here and that I was smart to come to her source.

At this point the nun perks up and insists that Guan Yin also lives in Canada. The monk disagrees and insists that Guan Yin is Chinese and therefore lives in China. The nun laughs and says that Guan Yin is Chinese but lives everywhere. I try to tell them that Guan Yin might not even be Chinese, but they either can't hear me over their arguing or don't care. Xiao Hesheng joins in, and Tino and I fade into the greenery.

"Are they arguing over whether or not Guan Yin is Chinese?" Tino asks.

"Yep. But I shouldn't laugh at them, Tino. Up until a couple of months ago I thought she was Chinese and lived in a house by the beach near here. And today I saw that very house..."

We stroll out of the square, down a lane where many colorful paper arrangements sit—I think they're used in funeral ceremonies. We pass several men and women in their pajamas. I'm happy to see that here on Putuo people behave the same way as in Chinese cities. It is a strange cultural phenomenon—pajama-wearing. But it happens across the country. Every night, men, women and children in various flannels and cottons—some striped, others with ducks or other cutesy animals—emerge from their houses. I see them milling about, washing their hair, smoking—all in their pajamas.

We reach the road and are about to turn back into town when I decide I need to see the empty Guan Yin house on the cliff. Tino says he'll accompany me, but I want to go by myself. The road is quiet, leading past the PLA base and up the hill to the dark turnoff toward the building. I walk confidently like I know where I'm going. My mind is still, not knowing what to expect.

The trees and shrubs are tall, lush with electric dusk light all over them—they throw dark blue shadows on the path. My feet don't feel like they're touching the ground as I approach the building with its delicate woodwork. It's two stories high and looks like it could lift off the earth, with soaring eaves on each corner of the roof.

A silence falls on me, but the waves below crash and roar. There's no one around, and I circle the building in its emptiness and then sit on the rock path in front of it. Part of me wonders if I might have seen this building in a photograph once and then thought I dreamed it or visualized it as Guan Yin's house. Another part of me knows quite well that I've never seen it in a photograph. And underlying both is the understanding that it doesn't matter either way. It doesn't matter if this was once my place—it isn't my place anymore—things have changed. I can't come to China looking for a rose-colored past any more than I can dream of a lofty future self in a future world. Like the nun said, Guan Yin doesn't live in a specific place; she lives wherever there is awareness, compassion and openness.

I close my eyes, perfectly calm here beside the deserted building above the sea. I sit for I don't know how long and have a strong sense of *zizai*—ease. I have a deep feeling of compassion for my trip here, for anyone else who's ever made a trip like this, and I feel as spacious as the sea that surrounds me.

Voices emerge from the foliage. It's Xiao Hesheng and the monk with bushy eyebrows and glasses. Night has fallen. Xiao Hesheng says I shouldn't be sitting here alone in the dark and they insist on escorting me home. As we walk, Xiao Hesheng and the other monk converse about something humorous and keep pausing to keel over and laugh. We make slow progress with their laughing. Although I have no idea what they're laughing about, it's contagious and I join in. We laugh so hard we're all gasping for breath. None of us knows what we're laughing about anymore. But it's terribly funny, whatever it is.

꧁

The boat ride back to Shanghai was about eighteen
hours, overnight. While the sun set and we motored
north, I sat on the deck with two Chinese fishermen
from a nearby island at which we stopped. They were
on their way to Shanghai to "play"—because the crabs
or whatever they fish for were all pregnant—so it was
not a good time for fishing. They said that they prayed
to Guan Yin every day while fishing and that she took
care of all the fishermen on the East Sea. We watched
the sun sink into the sea, then the sky turned electric
blue and then thick black.

I tried to sleep, but my designated bunk was in a room
full of snoring people and smelled like vomit. I spent
the night on deck outside, watching the blackness.

It began to rain near dawn as we pulled in from the
sea along the Pudong River toward Shanghai. Reeds and
willows lined the way and everything was enveloped in a
thin, mystical mist. Then came the swift navy boats, all
slick and gray. And then the ports: huge cranes load-
ing ocean liners with hundreds of containers heading
off to every country around the world. They went on
and on for two hours. Thousands and thousands of
containers filled with god knows what heading out to
the great seas.

Chapter 11

The Dissolution and the Arrest (Nanjing)
Yes Bar and how I got arrested during the Mid-Autumn Festival

Spring bled into summer and Nanjing became sultry. We hit a muggy forty-two degrees, and the only place to stay cool was the small lake on Zi Jin Shan. I bicycled there frequently, always returning after dark. The thick air was almost cool in the wind as my bike breezed past Ming tombs and lightless white cottages and glided into the frenzied center of Nanjing, alive with techno-blaring shops and fluorescent signs.

Summer stretched out like those night rides home. I explored mainly at night because by day it was too hot to venture out except for work at the radio station or my Mandarin classes. Liu Ming, my *qigong* teacher, moved to South America, but I still practiced *qigong* every night, in the park at the university. And then I practiced Gaelic football with the five other women from Nanjing who were on my team—the Shangahi Saints. We were preparing for the South Asian Cup. And then there was the street food—street parties where all the expatriates would gather at makeshift tables on colorful plastic stools and eat and drink beer under the milky summer sky and weak stars that managed to puncture Nanjing's haze.

It was at one of those events that I first noticed that I might be losing it. It was a particularly strange night because all of my expat friends were dressed in drag—we'd just left a party after being screamed at (with good cause) by the downstairs neighbors: a middle-aged Chinese couple who were sick of foreigners. We clattered out onto the street, me in a full suit, with my hair slicked back and with a greasy mustache. All my male friends were dressed in mini-skirts and bras. We made our way to the street where we always went to eat and ordered prawns, fried pumpkin cakes, noodles and fried vegetables. I sat with my back to the little creek of sludge that ran below the cooking stations on the side of the road beside the curb. Someone went into the supermarket and bought beer. We poured flimsy transparent cups full and began eating.

As things are in China, the sludge creek was also the depository for the shells of the prawns and at least a hundred of them already lay in a crunchy pile before we arrived. Quickly, our table added to them. I remember hearing the muted crunch of their bodies landing behind me as I ate my noodles. I remember thinking then about

Guan Yin—the myth of the two prawns who heard her teachings and became enlightened. In the myth they turn bad and use the teachings to wreak havoc on earth. I was thinking about all this as I reached for a beer. I leaned forward on my red plastic stool and grabbed the bottle. But as I sat down one of the legs buckled beneath me. I fell, fully aware, but unable to catch myself, backward and sideways into the sludge creek filled with prawn shells dressed as a man in a three-piece suit.

Then there was Yes Bar. I watched Yes Bar's construction from the street over my first two years here in Nanjing and swore I'd never visit. And then I did. My roommate Simon often went to Yes Bar with his Chinese associates. He said it was a good opportunity to "practice his Chinese" and "make connections." Not to mention he regularly picked up pretty young Chinese girls who believed that he would marry them and take them out of this country. He dated them two or three times and spent hours text messaging them before moving to another girl. His behavior, similar to that of many expat men in China, was an ongoing point of contention in our apartment. With regard to Yes Bar, Simon insisted that I was judging the place before I even experienced it. I couldn't argue with that. One night I just decided to go to Yes Bar. I remember having the thought, "How does one know summer's color unless one visits the garden?"

At Yes Bar's front door there is a hostess and six welcoming girls in long red dresses with slits up both legs to their waists. The stairs are curvy Cinderella steps of transparent glass, revealing a mosaic of sharp red and blue shards and luminous bulbs that lead toward the cabaret room. The walls drip with ornate glasswork and moldings. Everything in Yes Bar is curvier than it needs to be and sharper than it needs to be.

The color theme is inferno red and electric blue and not much in between. The two colors compliment each other the way only two ends of the spectrum can. It's a bar of extremes in a country of extremes—the birthplace of the yin and yang.

The cabaret room is packed. At least fifty tables on different levels hem the long serpentine sitting bar that in turn surrounds the T-shaped stage. The audience is made up of dark-suited businessmen with a few tables of more fashionable Nanjingers. Two thirds of the crowd is male, but there are plenty of couples smoking in the crowd.

At the back of the cabaret room is another long bar crowded with bartenders and a Red Army of "cowgirls" with bright ten-gallon hats and tiny red dresses. There's a special on: buy five beers and get the sixth free. Everyone seems to order six or twelve-packs of Tsing Tao or Bud and the beers grow warm as they sit on the table, waiting to be consumed.

A fat man in a dark suit sings cover songs from behind a furry microphone. After a hearty applause, people begin placing beers on the stage with 100-yuan bills stuffed in the necks. The man picks up one beer after another, pulls out the bill, holds it in his left hand while he chugs the beer. This is met with applause each time. He chugs four beers, pockets 400 yuan and then tears off his shirt. His chest is sweaty and hairless. People stand up, whoop and clap as he takes off his belt, swings it around his head and then wraps it around his chest—shiny patent leather on sweaty skin. He buckles it around the barrel of his chest so that it covers his nipples and breaks into another cover song.

Turning away from the fat man, I make my way to the back of the cabaret room, expecting to bump into Simon. I can't find him anywhere. Instead of attempting to walk through the crowd again, I take the back route through a hallway lined with plush benches, gilded mirrors and opaque doors leading to private karaoke and god-knows-what-else rooms.

The walls of Yes Bar's private halls are inset with rounded glass chips in intricate designs. It all feels futuristic and sinister. I turn the corner and run into ten young women wearing long semi-formal dresses in various pastel colors. They stand quietly, looking out of place in such a low-lit world. I smile and they smile back. A naive part of me hopes that they are there as a school group, renting a karaoke room and singing for each other. But as I round the next bend and find another group of young women in pastel dresses, my heart sinks. I'm used to seeing people standing around in China so their loitering doesn't distress me—it's what they are waiting for that does. They are not schoolgirls.

Prostitution may have been outlawed during Mao's reign, but it seems to be thriving in China now. There are plenty of late-night "hairdressers" here in Nanjing that will give you more than a haircut if you pay for it. I know that many businessmen and professionals "bond" in brothels or environments like this. I have a lawyer friend in Shanghai who is expected to go out with his boss to a brothel once a week—it's part of his job.

I ask one of the "schoolgirls" if she's seen a tall Englishman. She knows exactly what room he's in—room 23. I find it easily enough and open the door to Simon, his friend Zhao and two of Zhao's co-workers sitting around a TV screen singing karaoke. It is unreasonably loud and they are all drunk. The table before them is covered in ornately arranged fruit, several packs of beer, peanuts, chicken feet, and other tidbits.

"You came!" yells Simon, letting out a large cloud of smoke. The other men stand to greet me and shake my hand with limp grips and bows. Simon is controlling the song-choosing device. Zhao takes it from him and tells me to choose a song. I have been through this enough to know that I have to sing something. It's not that I can't sing or even that I don't enjoy singing; it's just the limited repertoire in China that gets to me after a while. It's the Beatles (early Beatles, except "Hey Jude"), the Carpenters, John Denver, or the odd movie theme song by Celine Dion to choose from.

I choose a song in Chinese, the only one I know all the words to, and take a piece of papaya. I am wondering what exactly I am doing here as Zhao sits beside me performing dice tricks. I feign interest until Simon hands me a beer to hide behind. I've met Zhao before, and he is always very kind to me. I don't know exactly what he does for a living, but apparently he works for the bank *and* the police and has an enormous expense account, the kind you'd expect a banker-policeman to have.

"Now don't get mad, but they've asked for some assistance," Simon says.

"What do you mean 'assistance'?" I ask.

"Well, some help with the karaoke machine," he says.

"Why would that make me mad?"

"You'll see," he smiles.

About a minute later the hostess comes in and speaks to Zhao. Then it begins. The door is propped open and the girls in pastel dresses come in one by one to be assessed by Zhao and the other men.

"They're choosing which girls they want to help with the machine," says Simon.

I am dumbstruck. I feel like a jerk sitting there with a bunch of communist banker-policemen and Simon while the girls are paraded through and assessed. I poke Zhao. "Tamen dou keyi, dou piaoliang," I tell him.

I don't know if he has noticed my discomfort but he quickly picks three girls and sends the rest away, giving the hostess a wad of 100-yuan bills.

The girl in the pale blue dress and long silky hair takes charge of the machine, while another, in white with her hair up, sings a recognizable song. The banker-policemen sing along with her. The third girl, in yellow, sits between Simon and me and asks us where we're from, how old we are and whether we are married. She is nineteen, from a town nearby, and is not married. I give Simon a dirty look.

"I know it's strange," he says. "But I've seen it worse. You know that fat one—last time he was making the girls sit on his lap and trying to put his hand up their shirts." He gestures to the fat banker-policeman.

"And you just sat there?" I growl.

"What was I supposed to do?" he asks.

The girl in blue hands me the microphone. It's my turn to sing: "The Moon Represents My Heart"—a sweet Taiwanese song that is nearly out of my register; I have to sing part of it falsetto. I sing, watching the words on the karaoke video of a girl and boy falling in love on a faraway beach. I finish to general applause. The girl in yellow begins to sing another song and the banker-policemen sing with her. I stand up and say goodbye.

"Where are you going then?" Simon complains.

"To watch the cabaret," I say.

Just outside of the cabaret room, a woman is sitting slumped over on a chair with a man's suit jacket over her head. She is drunk or strung out on something. Her dress, striped black and gray, is long and pools on the floor. I look at her for a few seconds and want to ask her if she's okay, but something prevents me.

The cabaret room is even more packed than when I first arrived. People are standing against the far wall behind tables, dry ice wisps over the stage and blue lights pulse overhead. I order a beer from one of the cowgirl waitresses. Simon finds me a minute later—even he is tired of the karaoke room antics.

"This place is mad!" he says, pointing to a man carrying the woman I have seen slumped over in the hallway. He takes her right past us, with her lolling eyes and rubber body. We watch, silent, as a path opens up in the crowd toward the front entrance. But the man turns and places her on the stage.

The woman opens her eyes and rolls backward onto the middle of the stage. She throws off the jacket, revealing a tiny red bra and the full length of her dress—which isn't a dress but a snake suit with a long, pointy tail. The crowd cheers. The dry ice puffs and the lights change to red. She begins a writhing gymnastic snake dance to a Middle Eastern flute song with a techno beat. Her eyes seem embedded in the back of her head; I can see only the whites as she slithers in our direction. The men beside us, all dressed in dark golf shirts and pleated pants, stand on their chairs to get a better view. They clutch each other in fear and expectation.

The lights change to blue with a strobe as she pulls off her snake suit, leaving only a red G-string. She is much more agile without her snake skin and performs headstands and splits. The dry ice puffs again and the man who carried her in opens a box and pulls out a snake. It's about an inch and a half thick and at least five feet long. He slides it along the stage where it crashes into the side of the woman's leg. She picks it up and dances, twirling it around and between her legs and smacking it against her back. It bites her.

The man pulls out another snake and slides it down the stage. Snake number 2 is even thicker than the first. She has one in each hand, twirling snake number 2 around and slapping it against her back where snake number 1 continues to bite her.

Snake number 3 arrives quickly and isn't as thick as the first two but seems to be much longer. It gets into a fight with snake number 1, but the snake lady remedies this by slapping them both against her back.

"Oh, that's sick," Simon yells as snake number 3 begins to pee creamy yellow ooze. The crowd screams again.

The dance finishes, the snakes are placed back in their box, and the snake lady is carried off the stage to a standing ovation. It seems like many people have come to see the snake show because there is an exodus of sorts after the act has ended. I feel like a camera, just watching. Simon orders some more beer and the warmth of drunkenness surrounds me.

A few minutes later, a woman in a white suit with tails strolls onstage. She must be six feet tall and reminds me of Meat Loaf. I'm waiting for her to start singing "Bat Out of Hell," but she doesn't. She sings a cover song with great gusto. The audience seems to like her because people keep approaching the bar with 100-yuan bills tucked into beers. The woman repeats the chugging technique of the man earlier in the evening and downs two beers. After chugging her third, she dances a funny kind of cha-cha, accentuating her large white form. The crowd laughs and she laughs. She pulls a tiny man from the audience and dances with him. At the end of the song she dips him backward and the crowd goes wild.

More beers flow toward the stage with 100-yuan bills tucked into them. The woman chugs her fourth beer and then twirls around with fierce speed. A techno beat kicks in and she bursts into song. Only it isn't a song, it's the Om Mani Padme Hum mantra—Guan Yin's mantra in Tibetan, meaning "Oh thou jeweled lotus!" She sings the line over and over again in a high-pitched voice. Many of the audience members also sing. I just sit there, dumbfounded. The line between the sacred and the profane has finally been blurred in my mind.

I think that it was probably at that moment that my discernment dissolved for good. Here I'd spent years forming a cohesive idea of what spiritual was—where it lived—like my idea that Guan Yin lived on Putuo or in pristine monasteries and in purple bamboo groves. And, of course, after my visit there it was clear that she did not—at least not in the form that I expected. And then there was the whole notion of her being a verb—not a noun—and that presented a more immediate necessity for me to take responsibility for my own mind and actions and for me to be Guan Yin, or Guan Zi Zai, rather than look for her.

And then there was Yes Bar, and my fumbling onto this large, white-tuxedoed form of Meat Loaf Lady singing *Om Mani Padme Hum*. Was I at ease watching that? Would I ever be the same after witnessing it? How does one act when all actions are to be Ease? Do you make rules—precepts saying, "This is ease; this isn't ease"? That's just the same as saying, "This is Guan Yin; this isn't." And how do I really know which is which? I know from experience that sometimes what I think is and what actually is do not match.

I can't draw a line through existence—and my life—and say, "This is spiritual; this isn't," or I'm setting myself up for an even bigger disillusion. So I accepted the Meat Loaf Guan Yin—I let her song ring through me; it was a sickly beautiful feeling. I went home after her act ended, and Yes Bar became a regular haunt throughout summer and into autumn.

Oh, autumn! Mid-Autumn Festival approached—as it had each year during my stay in China—with mooncakes showing up everywhere. Fruit-flavored, beef-flavored, bean-paste-flavored mooncakes. They always appeared in September and were cheap at the street vendors or expensive if you wanted designer mooncakes in glossy boxes. I ate many mooncakes and waited for the night of the Harvest Moon, when everyone in China takes to the streets to moon gaze and to celebrate the moon's splendor.

Mid-Autumn Festival happened to fall on the same night as the graduation party of some of my Australian friends in Nanjing. They'd just finished their course in traditional Chinese medicine and invited me to the celebrations. We enjoyed a big dinner and lots of wine and then headed out to the roof of the hotel to watch the moon.

The giant exhaust on the roof kept coughing out clouds of damp laundry-smelling steam, making the autumn night muggy. We drank a couple more of bottles of wine and looked at the moon. I got fairly drunk and started singing, "The Moon Represents My Heart" at the top of my voice over the rooftops. It was a concert of sorts, with some of the university's administrators standing on the ground watching us.

Then someone suggested we go to Yes Bar. There were probably twenty of us scattered through the place, some watching the cabaret, others in the basement disco bar dancing in cages and spinning in the strobe lights. I was upstairs in the cabaret room with two friends—Mary-Jo and Daniel, both new doctors and both at least as drunk as I was. Mary-Jo was a very intelligent blond-haired and blue-eyed Tasmanian. Daniel was a sometimes boisterous, sometimes brooding Russian-Australian who was thinking of becoming an Orthodox monk. He reminded me of Alexie, the youngest brother of the Karamazovs —good-natured like him, but brooding, like a proper

Russian. The three of us had been frequenting bars in recent months, and Mary-Jo was on my Gaelic football team. Daniel and I practiced *qigong* twice a week in the park.

On the stage, a small man sang romantic love songs. Mary-Jo, Daniel, and I drank and watched him. "This guy is boring," said Mary-Jo after a time. But it looked like most of the audience, particularly the couples out celebrating romantic Mid-Autumn eve, enjoyed his singing. Then the man began a lilting rendition of "The Moon Represents My Heart," and the next thing I knew, Daniel and I were waltzing on stage in front of the entire audience. We danced the whole song through and received a standing ovation. The singer entered into another whiny love song, and I saw a glaze of boredom pass across everyone's face. It didn't take long for someone to suggest that we go outside and watch the moon. We filed out of Yes Bar and made our way back up the street. We didn't walk more than thirty feet before a car came up behind us honking.

"Get off the sidewalk; you're in a car," I said to the driver.

"Fuck you!" he retorted and kept driving toward us. We got out of the way.

And then my reason deserted me. I gave the car a good solid kick on the driver's door. I could feel adrenaline flowing in my bloodstream. And by the time we made it to the corner, the man whose car I kicked was upon us. He grabbed me first, but I used a tai chi move to loosen his arm. So he grabbed Mary-Jo. Within a minute a crowd had assembled around us. I don't know where they all came from. They began pushing and probing. Most of them men. All of them were drunk.

The crowd got rougher and yelling began. Daniel was clearly the largest male in the area, and he quickly became the crowd's main target. Several of the group started roughing him up. A few of our friends from Yes Bar were on the periphery, trying to break through. I could hear a Taiwanese student, Mike, trying to diffuse the situation, although his Taiwanese accent seemed to make things worse. Voices in the crowd yelled, "Taiwanese, Taiwanese!"

The next thing I knew, fists were flying. Daniel yelled, "Run!"

I ran. Mary-Jo ran, Daniel ran, up the street, through a dark gate and into some bushes. I had never been so scared in my life. My throat was dry. I could barely speak. Mary-Jo was shaking, and we didn't know what happened to Daniel or Mike.

༚

The police station, like so many government buildings in China, felt empty. There was minimal furniture, nothing on the walls and a general sterility and lack of humanity to the place. Mr. Hao, the police sergeant, took Mary-Jo and me to a small, bare room with wooden chairs. We had to make a statement. Mr. Hao had a round face and the curly hair that few Chinese people possess. Daniel was there. He had a swollen eye and a goose egg forming on his head. Someone had thrown a bike at him and he lost his crucifix during the brawl. He told us that Mike was okay but was being questioned separately because he was Taiwanese.

I felt nauseous and nearly puked at the station. Mary-Jo cried. Despite the friendliness I experienced in Nanjing, there is an underlying dislike and mistrust of foreigners. Just the month before, my friend Steven was beaten with a broken bottle and left lying unconscious in an alley outside a nightclub in Nanjing by a group of guys that thought he was using Chinese women. The irony was that Steven is gay.

Nonetheless, there are lots of Westerners that do exploit Chinese women. And people like me, who should have probably left several months earlier and are foolish enough to kick cars. The Chinese population isn't stupid—they can see the transformation that's taking place in their society and likely want a piece of the pie that Westerners are so often privy to here.

We completed our statements. Mr. Hao said that everything would be okay if I agreed to pay 600 yuan for the damages to the car. I agreed. We took a taxi home, and I fell into a troubled sleep.

That was last night. Today is a day of waiting. I've been nauseous all day, and the only thing I can stomach is red licorice. So I've been eating red licorice and stale mooncakes, waiting for Mr. Hao to call and ruminating on how I got myself into this situation. I'm eager to pay my fine and get on with life, but I can't shake the feeling that I should have left China a few months ago. My life feels rudderless, ridiculous this morning. And I drank too much last night—I have a raging hangover. The Tibetan mystics called alcohol "Crazy Black Water," and I think they were right.

At 5:00 Mr. Hao calls. There's a complication. I need to come to the police station immediately and bring my passport. Daniel and Mike are also coming, but Mary-Jo has been absolved from the meeting.

We gather around a large oval table with a hole in the center, where a couple of plants sit. The room has several windows overlooking the rooftop and nearby apartments. The city looks unfamiliar to me from this perspective. My body is numb, my stomach sick, my throat dry.

Several policemen sit across the table from Daniel, Mike, the translator and me. I notice that friendly Mr.

Hao is not present. Another man is in charge. He's wearing a white golf shirt and has a crooked smile. The other policemen are in uniform and don't smile.

The first person they interrogate is Mike. Apparently he's being charged with making "anti-Chinese statements" and inciting the street brawl. I pipe up and say that I started everything by kicking the car and that he was trying to diffuse the situation because he can speak fluent Mandarin. They don't seem to hear me. Mike is lead to a small room where he will remain until he writes a confession admitting to saying "anti-Chinese statements" and a formal apology to the Chinese people.

"This is ridiculous!" I say.

"This is China," Mike says as he disappears through the door.

The translator fills Daniel's and my cups with water and green tea leaves. The leaves float to the surface. I watch them, like they might offer some insight. Then Mike's words sink in, and it dawns on me that I am in China and subject to Chinese law. The golf-shirt-man pulls out a plastic bag and dangles it across the table at us. There's a gold watch inside.

"This Rolex watch was damaged in the street fight. The owner wants compensation for it," he says.

He passes the watch to the policeman beside him who walks it around the table and gives it to Daniel. On closer examination, the watch appears to have been hit with a hammer. The face is shattered and the little hands are bent and broken with no hope of ever turning again.

"First of all, who in that brawl could afford a Rolex? And secondly, there's no way in hell that that watch was smashed on someone's arm!" I say, full of righteous anger.

"Yeah, they would have a broken arm if it were. Please show us the arm this watch was broken on," says Daniel.

The translator is more eloquent than Daniel and me in Chinese and translates our case to the police. The man in the golf shirt seems to almost agree with us, but he doesn't back down. Instead, he asks for our passports and says that we have been placed under city arrest until the issue is resolved. He says that he'll personally look into the fact of the broken watch and cost for repair.

I tell him that I have to leave China to renew my visa and play a football match in Hong Kong. He tells me that he'll renew my visa and that I won't be going to Hong Kong to play football. Two policemen escort us out of the station and instruct us to stay home. They will call us with an update in the next couple of days. Daniel and I drift up the street, frightened, paranoid. The city feels sinister—even familiar intersections and lanes have lost their innocence.

I go home and do the only thing I know will ease my mind—I pack. I pack up all my possessions, take them to the post office and mail them to Canada. If I can't leave, at least my things can.

I live in an empty room for two days—I'm afraid to leave the apartment. There is a lens on everything, nausea. I wake in the middle of the night with surges of adrenaline flooding my chest, flooding my arms. They come at regular intervals like a wave and then disappear like the receding tide only to wash in again a few minutes later. I plan escape routes across the Himalayas. By boat. But then I remember Daniel and Mike—I can't very well abandon them here in this mess. Daniel invites me over and orders Indian food. He tries to make me eat, but I can't swallow anything except red licorice.

After two days the phone rings. It's Mr. Hao, the friendly police sergeant. He wants me to come to the police station. He has some bad news. I call Daniel and we plan to go together.

On my way out the door I remember the 3000 yuan I have hidden in my closet. It's payment I received for adjudicating a provincial speech competition. The competition itself is an example of how China plays by different rules than I do: the guy who hired me as a judge for the competition was actually a contestant. What's more, he had me edit his speech and help him with pronunciation before the competition. I wasn't the only judge, so the fact that he won can't be attributed to me alone. But it must have looked strange when after the competition he paid me while I was still sitting at my judge's booth. And he asked me to count the 3000 yuan in front of everyone to ensure it was all there.

I slip the 3000 yuan into my bag in hopes that I can bribe my way out of China. Mike, Daniel and I meet Mr. Hao in his private office. He looks sad.

"I'm sorry, but the man whose Rolex watch was broken has overridden our jurisdiction and taken the case to the provincial court. There's nothing that we at the police station can do now. We agree with you that it doesn't seem fair, but you have been called to provincial court in three months' time and will be tried under Chinese laws. You are not permitted to leave the country."

I didn't think the situation could get any worse. I feel a weak surge of adrenaline, overpowered by a numbing fear. I've heard that ninety percent of defendants in China end up being found guilty in Chinese courts. Innocent people have admitted to murder under the strain and coercion of the system.

Mr. Hao gives us our passports back and we leave the station in silence. I pause at the curb, not knowing what to say, how to apologize for the situation we've landed in. Everyone looks exhausted. Evening has fallen and the sky is murky blue. We decide to call our respective consulates, but before we can cross the street a car pulls up in front of us. It's a small black car with tinted windows. Two men hop out. They wear official uniforms and speak to us directly. They're from the provincial court. They both point to their chest pins. I move closer for a look and see that the pins are red miniature scales of justice that swing back and forth. It seems almost too literal to be true. I want to laugh but don't dare. Mike speaks to them in Chinese.

"They want us to come to the courthouse and meet a judge and settle out of court," says Mike. "Do you want to?"

"Yes."

The three of us squish into the back seat of the car and drive north through the city to the provincial courthouse. It's a large, looming building, but with some class—granite and marble fittings. It's a far cry from the police station. The men with the scales of justice on their chests lead us to a room on the fourth floor. Another man, a judge, sits at the head of a long wooden table. We're offered seats in soft black leather chairs, and I begin to feel oddly comfortable in the courthouse.

The judge smiles at us. He also wears scales of justice on his chest, but his are slightly larger and a darker red. His suit is gray and he looks like a drinker—his face sort of red and round.

"Let the extortion begin," whispers Mike, who for some reason is finding this highly amusing. I'm encouraged by his humor.

A lawyer representing the man whose car I kicked and whose watch we supposedly broke arrives. He's a small, rat-like thing, probably in his late twenties and positively terrified of the situation. He hands us each a statement about the car kicking and watch breaking. Apparently there are several eyewitnesses to support his claim that we broke the watch during the brawl. They are requesting $10,000 for compensation.

Mike laughs out loud. He laughs so loud that I start laughing. Pretty soon Daniel joins in, and I can even see a twinkle in the judge's eye.

"Tell him that I'll give him 2000 yuan for the dent in the car," I say with my opening bargain.

"Nice," Mike says. "Low and tough. We'll see what we come back with." We grow more comfortable in our leather chairs.

The little lawyer returns a few minutes later with a response: 4500 yuan.

"See, I told you they were bluffing. From 10,000 dollars to 4500 yuan in one bargain!" laughs Mike.

"Tell them I'll pay 2200 yuan," I say confidently. I feel like my two years of bargaining for everything in China is finally paying off.

The little lawyer disappears again. The judge looks impressed and pleased at the efficiency of the situation. He tells one of the men who brought us here to pour everyone some tea. I begin to realize that they're probably relieved as well to have this under control.

The lawyer returns with a firm 2500 yuan. I don't miss a beat. I take 25 crisp red Chairman Mao bills out of my purse, count them on the table and hand them to the little lawyer. We each sign a document. The judge stamps it and everyone smiles.

"Extortion complete!" Mike pronounces, first in English, then in Chinese. Everyone laughs except for the little lawyer. Daniel stands up and growls at the lawyer and he flees. The judge reminds us to stay out of trouble as we exit the courthouse. We promise to. I feel like I can fly as we pile into the back of the tinted-windowed car and chat to the court men in their matching suits and charming scales of justice swinging on their breasts.

Chapter 12

Farewell to China (Guizhou)

A small terraced village where I love China once more

Whenever I travel by train in China, I always pay a little extra so that I can have a bottom bunk. The bottom bunks are the only ones where you can sit upright. There's an unspoken courtesy that during the day the people on the bunks above are allowed to sit on the edge of the bottom bunk or the two foldout chairs by the window to eat or socialize. I've always found train travel to be fairly pleasant and consistently met interesting and friendly people on trains during my time in China.

On the train in Shanghai, Annalise and I make our way through the car toward our bunks and round the corner to find my bunk occupied by a man who has obviously spent the night sleeping on it. He likely boarded somewhere in the north and has made himself at home, reclining shirtless, in his small white shorts, chewing on a chicken leg. I explain to him that the bottom bunk is in fact mine. I show him my ticket that states clearly that I have "xia"—or lower bunk. But he doesn't care. He continues to lie there in the sticky heat, half naked, dripping chicken juice down himself.

Maybe my eyes have grown fiery, but I can feel Annalise's hand on my arm. "Don't get into a fight with him. It's not worth it." She warns.

I can hear what she's saying, and I realize that it's good common sense, but my ears are beginning to ring and I want to take that chicken leg and shove it up his nose. I tell him that he has no manners and he screams back, "Stupid egg foreigner," and various other insults.

Annalise doesn't speak enough Chinese to understand what he's saying, so she can blessedly ignore greasy chicken man as he grunts and complains and picks up his giblets and moves over so that I can sit on my bunk beside him. I unpack some things and try to make myself at home.

After a time, the train starts up and greasy chicken man finishes his meal and moves over to the window seat. But he takes the opportunity to tell everyone in the immediate vicinity what a terrible foreigner I am and how rude I was to him. He goes on and on for what seems like an eternity.

"Just ignore him," says Annalise. "It's probably some kind of karmic test. Ignore him." She's still scared that

I might start another confrontation. Annalise was a traditional Chinese medicine student in Nanjing and was around when the brawl and arrest happened. She has bright green eyes, a good sense of humor and is well traveled. I lie down on my bunk, cover my head with a T-shirt and try to ignore greasy chicken man, who is still going on. I can feel my blood boiling as the train pulls us south.

I have so many emotions in me, they feel like chemicals in my bloodstream: anger, fear—and the pulse of adrenaline that my body's grown accustomed to. I let it wash over me in waves. I visualize light and watch my breath. I say Guan Yin's name.

What if Annalise is right? What if this man is a test—a final test for me here in China? He's easily the most annoying person I've ever met—it's like he's been appointed to drive me crazy. What if he is Guan Yin? I decide to let him say whatever he likes. I'm not going to react anymore. I listen to him bark away every so often at whoever will listen and I eventually fall asleep. Awaking, I find him gone. He's moved up to his own bunk.

Annalise smiles at me from across the table. "Looks like you passed the test," she says. The landscape streams by, and I have the feeling that I might actually make it out of China in one piece.

꧁꧂

The train to Guizhou took over twenty-four hours. I spent most of it in reverie, reliving the past week—the car kicking, the police, how a life can change in an instant, what I'm going to do next. Annalise is convinced that here in Guizhou we'll finally see the picturesque China everyone comes looking for. Then we'll continue on to Laos and finally India.

All I really want to do is leave China. But here I am in Guizhou. Guizhou is one of those Chinese provinces that foreigners don't visit. There's nothing to mention about the cities, and the whole province is kind of in the middle of nowhere in the southwest of China. The only thing I've ever read about Guizhou was that during the Long March, this was a province where Mao and his followers snaked up and down, confusing the Gumingdong army with constant movement. And there was a saying that in Guizhou, "There aren't three *li* without a mountain, no three days without rain, and you won't find anyone with three pieces of silver on them." For generations the province was chock-full of opium addicts, everyone was poor, and many of the minority people didn't even have clothes.

Actually, there is one other thing I've heard about Guizhou: that during the Cultural Revolution, there were several hundred accounts of ritual cannibalism recorded here. So based on my knowledge about the province, I admit that I've never had any desire to visit it. But we decide to stay for a few days, and I let myself move deeper into the belly of China.

We stroll around Leishan's muddy bus station reading signs on the fronts of buses and eventually find one to Xijiang. We pile in along with about twenty other people, many of them cultural minorities—I can tell by their clothes—traditional—and their faces—not quite Han. Several large sacks of clothes and grains and three chickens complete the cargo and we're off.

Moving out of the city, the countryside quickly turns picturesque—emerald hills and dark wood houses with gray-tiled roofs and bird's wing eves. The haystacks are cone-shaped with pointy tops. Men and women stand in the fields threshing grain into large baskets. My mind softens with the landscape. Ease permeates me, and despite my misgivings about coming here, I begin to enjoy Guizhou.

After an hour or so, the valleys deepen and our road turns to dirt, becoming treacherous as it winds its way deeper into the misty landscape. Eventually, the valley reveals a village and everyone on the bus brightens. Dipping down to Xijiang feels like a homecoming. In every direction there are terraced fields and traditional houses scattered up the mountainside, many with long strings of colorful dried corn and bright red peppers draped across them like vegetable Christmas lights.

As we pull into the main street, the woman sitting beside us pokes me. She has bright eyes, speaks Mandarin, and invites us to come and stay at her house for as long as we like for 10 yuan a day, meals included. We agree. Mist huddles around the buildings as we ascend the stairs toward Lili's house. It's mainly people of the Miao minority group who inhabit the town. Their houses are made of hardwood, maybe maple, built on stilts, with fowl and pigs beneath. Lili explains that none of the houses are built directly in front of others so that when the spirits of the ancestors return they have a clear path.

"I hope they don't return tonight when we're sleeping," Annalise says. I shiver. Though beautiful, there's something eerie about these hills. Imagine the architects considering the ghosts of ancestors while positioning a house. I feel like I've walked into another country—a lifetime away from the communist courtroom the other night. But I'll take ancestor ghosts over communist administrators any day.

Dinner at Lili's house is a hot pot of vegetables and meat served in the center of the living room. Liu, her husband, entertains us and insists that we try some homemade liquor—he has a vat of it in the entranceway and pours it into a small decanter so that it's manageable. The cups are small and deep blue. Before drinking, we have to offer a few drops of liquor to the ancestors by pouring some from each cup onto the floor. The liquor is strong, fruity and burns the whole way down. Liu empties his cup; Annalise and I follow suit. This makes him very happy. He refills our cups and tells us about how Chairman Mao's grandmother was of the Miao minority—that's why Chairman Mao was so smart and strong.

Liu practices kung fu and has photos of himself on the wall doing fancy moves. We get into a discussion about qi and *qigong* and before long, he and I are in the middle of the floor doing push hands like we're old friends. He's a wiry man, but flexible and strong.

Lili's niece arrives—she's about twelve years old and has wide eyes and a mischievous smile. I like her immediately. She sits beside me and sings a song about how Chinese girls are the prettiest. I get my audio recorder and have her sing it again. I play it back for her and for the first time in her life she hears her own voice. She plays the song over and over again, singing along with herself, and I have to agree with the lyrics—Chinese girls are the prettiest.

Liu has decided that Annalise and I are suitable drinking companions for the night, so he keeps filling up our cups. These tiny Chinese cups are always deceiving, particularly when they're never left empty for more than a few seconds. Before long, Liu has to refill the decanter. Annalise and I giggle and melt into the old couch. The room is bare except for the few photographs of Liu in his kung fu outfit and one of him and Lili at their wedding. But this is a happy room. These people seem genuinely happy with so little. I let out a sigh of contentment.

"China goes sour in an instant and in an instant redeems itself," Annalise muses.

"Indeed," I admit. I feel like I'm falling in love with China once more. This country of paradoxes, of great heights and profound depths never ceases to amaze me. And the more of Liu's homemade liquor I drink, the more I can feel the anxiousness of the past week melt away. Night is falling on the village, the mist has disappeared and stars are visible outside the wide window.

Every few minutes another friend or relative arrives in the living room; I don't know where they're all coming from. Many of them are in their thirties—the same age as Liu and Lili—but some older people also trickle in. The circle around the table expands to include everyone, the decanter has to be refilled constantly, and our tiny cups are never empty for long. The floor is soaked; I'm confident the ancestors are as drunk as we.

"I bet the ancestors will have a hard time finding their way home if they drink any more!" I laugh. Annalise laughs and everyone else laughs, although they don't know what I'm saying.

The room begins to sway. All the faces have a soft blur around them. Next thing I know, six women stand before us in full traditional garb—silver coronets on their heads, silky sleeves and silver bells on their chests. They sing for us with their ancestors' booze moist beneath their feet. There is a tinge of longing in the song that somehow fits in with this misty, isolated landscape. My chest fills with love for this little village and these people.

The women disappear and Liu pours more drinks for us to cheer their fine performance. Annalise and I are beginning to slow down in our drinking—I don't know how many decanters we've emptied, but the room is certainly spinning.

Lili mentions my guitar—she carried it up the hill for me from the bus stop. She asks if I will sing a Canadian song for everyone. I try and think of something traditional, but I don't know anything traditional from Canada—I can think only of Leonard Cohen, Joni Mitchell and Neil Young, some of Canada's best songwriters. They might not be too far from the folk tunes sung by women in matching traditional outfits up a mountain. I choose Neil Young's "Heart of Gold." I translate the title into Mandarin and everyone agrees that a golden heart is worth looking around the world for.

Everyone claps and sways along with the song. The song is a hit. And it seems to be the finale of the night. Liu has stopped pouring alcohol and people are disappearing as mysteriously as they arrived. Annalise and

I tumble into the bedroom, the walls spinning around us.

"I love China," I say decidedly.

"Me too," says Annalise. She opens the window and vomits over the narrow valley and silent houses.

Chapter 13

꧁

Standing Buddha Caves (Laos)
A visit to Pak Ou's Standing Buddha Caves and Pocket Guan Yin

China has long arms. It stretches further than it probably should—Tibet, Inner Mongolia, Xinjiang (with its large Muslim population), Taiwan's waters, all the way to Afghanistan and Pakistan. The trip south through Xixuanbana into Laos was a good illustration: out the bus window the landscape turned lush and jungley, the faces brown and soft; the architecture changed to flaming roofed houses and temples in the South Asian style, the writing on the buildings to wispy alphabets instead of Chinese characters—but it was still China. This went on for hundreds of kilometers. At one point I wondered if China would ever end or if I were trapped in some strange dream.

I did the only thing I could do then. I stretched out on the bus and fell asleep while China stretched further south until its border finally arrived. Annalise snapped my picture as I crossed the threshold into Laos. We made it to Luang Prabhang without much hassle and have spent our first days out of China eating coconut curry dishes beside the Mekong River and acting like proper tourists.

Luang Prabhang is the ancient capital of Laos. For more than eight centuries, this city was the home of the king and the cultural center of the kingdom. It's been sacked and burned several times, and its most recent incarnation has a distinct French feel since most of the houses and shops were built in French colonial style. The Mekong curves beside the city, moist jungle surrounds it, and right in the center of town sits Mount Phousi. The city has many temples with soaring roofs, shiny imbedded glass dragons, bodhisattvas, elephants and flowers, and it is peopled by saffron-clothed monks and Western tourists.

Luang Prabhang is also the "home of the standing Buddha." I read that somewhere. I don't know whether it's true or not, but I like the idea. I've always been drawn to standing Buddha and bodhisattva images—they look like they're up to something. I wonder how it was that here in this little city in the middle of the jungle, Buddhism arrived and, iconographically, the Buddhas started to stand. There's an entire cave upstream from Luang Prabhang that is supposedly filled with standing Buddhas and bodhisattva statues.

Considering my quest to find Guan Yin in China has ended with my arrest and untimely departure, I decided yesterday that the best way to end my trip to the Far East is to take a boat upstream to the Standing Buddha Caves and leave my Pocket Guan Yin there. The decision to leave her there came quite naturally while I was sitting by the river yesterday. I realize that my whole journey to the East looking for Guan Yin the Boddhisattva of Compassion has actually been a lesson in letting go. Letting go and seeing what comes in to fill the space created. Besides, I need some closure to my time in China, and what better way than leaving her there in the caves as testament to my understanding that Guan Yin is not a physical being—she is symbolic of a way of being—being at ease, being open, the kind of ease and openness that eludes me most of the time.

I slept with the small statue of Guan Yin in my hand last night and awoke clutching her tiny form like a child would a stuffed toy. I awoke semi-paralyzed because I thought I was still in China under city arrest, and then I felt slightly embarrassed that I was laying in the darkness clinging to a tiny wooden statue. I wondered: why do hands curl naturally if not to hold on to something? And if that is so, why do humans spend so much time learning to let go? I went out onto the balcony, placed Pocket Guan Yin on the railing and watched the milky pink sunrise over the Mekong River.

Luang Prabhang wakes slowly, almost like a resort town. There were probably hundreds of monks doing morning oblations in the temples and hundreds of workers digging somewhere, but from my vantage point over the river, the town was still—the perfect place to contemplate what I'm going to do with myself now that I've left China. But I couldn't see past today. So I decided to start the day. I had a cold shower and went to the restaurant on the river for a red curry breakfast with Annalise and two guys we met on the bus to Luang Prabhang, Martin and Dave. Martin is a photographer from Germany, working his way around the world. He used to be a drummer in a death-metal band and sports an enormous tattoo of the Grim Reaper on his shoulder. Dave is an astronomy student from Lethbridge, Alberta. He's taken up smoking and betting since he's been in Asia because they give him "something to do." He's tried to get me to bet him on several things already.

After breakfast the four of us make our way along the small French-housed road overlooking the Mekong. Ahead of us are several young monks. Luang Prabhang is full of teenaged saffron-robed monks. They come here from poor country towns and receive free education in the monasteries for three years. After that, many return to their villages, some stay on at the monasteries, and fewer still go on to higher education. The monks often travel in pairs or small groups, sometimes crowded under an umbrella for shade.

The monks ahead of us stop and wait. They're the same group we met yesterday and are eager to practice English. They escort us down the steep grassy slope knotted with jungley shrubs and flowers toward the dock. Two long, narrow boats bob in the water with room for about twenty to sit on rickety benches under flat roofs. The driver sits at the front of one boat with five Western tourists behind him. It looks like they've arranged an excursion similar to ours.

A woman in the boat wearing a large white hat greets us in a thundering voice: "You know those monks are all little perverts. One of them grabbed my ass the other day. You shouldn't go anywhere alone with them." Her friends all nod. "I thought they were spiritual people. No way. They're a bunch of perverts." She asks if we'd like to get into her boat instead of renting our own. We decline and hop into another boat. It's blue. The driver starts up the engine and we're off upstream.

Before Buddhism ever arrived in Laos, the Pak Ou caves were holy places for the Lao animist faith. Monks used to live in both the upper and lower caves, and locals still believe that good spirits inhabit them.

Several hundred years ago, people began bringing Buddha and bodhisattva images to the caves. Some people say that they bring the statues as offerings; others say it's because temples have closed and no one knows what to do with the statues. I picture a sort of retirement or retreat caves for statues—somewhere they can get together and observe the world's sounds or be at ease among like-minded beings.

I can't think of a better place to leave the little sandalwood Guan Yin. I've attempted to give her away twice now, but both times she was returned to me—once by an old monk in Tibet, the other time by my friend Matt, whose bag I put her in while he was heading to Australia.

I drag my hand in the water and watch my mind creep upstream toward China. The Mekong originates there. I try to drag my mind back to the present. Being present is the most important thing I've learned in all of my travels and research about Guan Yin—because that's where she is—in the hum of the engine, in the rippled water, in the lush jungle.

"This is the furthest south I've been," I tell Annalise.

"Yeah, this is my first time in the southern hemisphere too," says Dave.

"We're not in the southern hemisphere, Dave," says Annalise. "I'm from the southern hemisphere, and this isn't it."

"Of course we are," says Dave.

"No, we're not!" Martin laughs.

Dave gets serious. "Sarah. You've been in China for two-and-a-half years and just came really far south to get to Laos, right?" he asks. I nod. "So, we must be in the southern hemisphere because China is in the southern hemisphere."

"Are you kidding?" I have visions of Chinese borders next to Mongolia, Afghanistan and North Korea and laugh harder. Annalise suggests that we bet on it. Dave and I shake hands.

"10,000 kip we are in fact in the northern hemisphere," I say.

"10,000 kip we're in the southern hemisphere," he asserts.

This is my first bet for money, and I'm a little excited. Dave settles back in his chair, lights a cigarette. "You know I study astronomy and don't profess to be a geographer, but I think you two are wrong. Everyone knows that China is on the opposite side of the world as Canada—even children know that. Just think of Bugs Bunny cartoons. Have you ever seen the ones when he tunnels through the earth?" We nod. "Well, where does he end up?"

We are all speechless. "He ends up in China!" Dave proclaims.

I picture Bugs Bunny popping up in a rice patty field beside a small, black-clothed Chinese farmer in a large sun hat. Dave believes it, and nothing that Martin, Annalise or I can say will change his mind.

Only the lower cave is visible from the boat. Its entrance is wide, and from a distance I can see hundreds of little Buddhas and bodhisattvas peeking out over the river.

We pull up to a large dock beside two other boats. Climbing the stone stairs I hear a man complaining about the entrance cost to the caves: "This is a rip-off, 8000 kip to see a bunch of dusty old statues. I'm not going in!" The woman tending the gate neither speaks English nor seems to care about the man's protest. She stands at the gate staring off across the river, not unlike the Buddha statues behind her. We pay the equivalent of eighty cents and enter the mouth of the lower cave. It's tiered and not very deep, so most of the statues are bathed in soft browny-orange sunlight.

Martin has three cameras and begins taking photos of the army of Buddhas. Dave, Annalise and I creep around investigating the statues. Some of them are gathered around small clay stupas like they're having a meeting. Others stand alone in the corner beside colored flags that someone has painted. There are mini-altars set before a few groups with tiny garlands of flowers around their necks. Each statue is unique, and I find the whole scene welcoming and sweet—like a Buddha tea party or one of those gatherings in the sutras when all the Buddhas and bodhisattvas get together, and it rains flowers while they hold discourses on the meaning of existence.

"Don't you think it's strange that people give away their statues?" wonders Dave, his nose nearly touching an ochre-robed Buddha.

"Not really," I reply. I reach in my bag for Pocket Guan Yin.

"But, I mean, I don't believe in any of this stuff, but aren't these statues supposed to protect you?"

"Maybe the people who brought these statues have gone beyond the attachment to physical forms of the Buddha and bodhisattvas?" I ponder out loud, still looking for Guan Yin.

"What's a bodhisattva?" he asks.

"A *pusa*," I answer in Chinese, although he can't speak Chinese. I empty the contents of my bag on the steps. He gives me a confused look, mouths "pusa" at me and continues poking around the cave.

I can't believe it. Guan Yin is not in my bag. I try to retrace my steps this morning. I can't possibly have forgotten her. I never forget her. Maybe she got sick of me always trying to give her away and left me!

Deflated and abandoned, I pick up my things and sit down among a gang of bodhisattvas overlooking the Mekong. The light is so bright coming in now that they are silhouettes against the sparkling river. I blink and stare at their dark shapes until their outlines burn into my retina. I can see them with my eyes closed now, flickering electric blue green. What is a bodhisattva? If the Buddha is famous for getting liberated and leaving the three worlds, the bodhisattvas are famous for getting liberated and staying in the three worlds. They choose to stay. They let go and then hang on.

Martin and Annalise want to check out the upper cave, and I join them. We make our way up the hot green jungle path wrapping around the side of the mountain away from the river. The day is still and quiet. High-pitched summer quiet.

The entrance to the upper cave is black. Inside, the cave is even blacker, cool and damp. Martin has read a guidebook and has come prepared with a lighter and a red candle. He illuminates a small section of the cave as we walk through. It's deep and has bends. There are hundreds more statues on platforms and up the walls, casting huge shadows in the candlelight. In one corner behind a mound of stone is a Buddha's graveyard with little heads and broken arms in piles. Apparently many of the statues are several hundred years old; a lot of them are likely rotting or decomposing.

The cave has a meditative mood to it; it makes me want to sit. I find a spot around a corner, near the statue graveyard where there's no external light. I listen to Martin take long exposures of the statues. Annalise hums something unrecognizable in the distance.